D0538260

English Result

Elementary Workbook

Joe McKenna

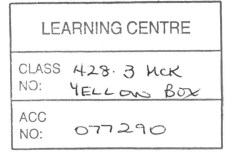
HARROW COLLEGE
HH Learning Centre
Lowlands Road, Harrow
Middx HA1 3AQ
020 8909 6520

O
UN

1 **Personal identification**

A How to **say hello**
>> p.4

B How to **say phone numbers & email addresses** >> p.5

C How to **give your name and address**
>> p.6

D How to **start a conversation**
>> p.7

Skills Practice >> pp.8–9

Self check 1 >> p.76

2 **Personal relations**

A How to **use English in the classroom**
>> p.10

B How to **introduce your family**
>> p.11

C How to **describe people**
>> p.12

D How to **talk about the time**
>> p.13

Skills Practice >> pp.14–15

Self check 2 >> p.77

3 **Countries and places**

A How to **ask for information**
>> p.16

B How to **talk about countries**
>> p.17

C How to **say where you are in town**
>> p.18

D How to **talk about language skills**
>> p.19

Skills Practice >> p.20–21

Self check 3 >> p.78

4 **Everyday life**

A How to **respond to news**
>> p.22

B How to **say dates**
>> p.23

C How to **describe habits**
>> p.24

D How to **describe a typical day**
>> p.25

Skills Practice >> pp.26–27

Self check 4 >> p.79

5 **Relations with others**

A How to **introduce people**
>> p.28

B How to **describe people and objects**
>> p.29

C How to **ask for things in shops**
>> p.30

D How to **ask about people's interests**
>> p.31

Skills Practice >> pp.32–33

Self check 5 >> p.80

6 **Food and drink**

A How to **ask about prices**
>> p.34

B How to **order food in a café**
>> p.35

C How to **talk about food**
>> p.36

D How to **offer things**
>> p.37

Skills Practice >> pp.38–39

Self check 6 >> p.81

7 Leisure and entertainment

A How to talk about free-time activities
>> p.40

B How to talk about the weather
>> p.41

C How to describe abilities
>> p.42

D How to talk about likes and dislikes
>> p.43

Skills Practice >> pp.44–45

Self check 7 >> p.82

8 Going out

A How to invite and reply
>> p.46

B How to say what to wear
>> p.47

C How to say what's happening
>> p.48

D How to describe actions
>> p.49

Skills Practice >> pp.50–51

Self check 8 >> p.83

9 Places, transport, and travel

A How to ask for transport information
>> p.52

B How to give and follow directions
>> p.53

C How to ask about and describe a holiday >> p.54

D How to tell a story
>> p.55

Skills Practice >> pp.56–57

Self check 9 >> p.84

10 Personal histories

A How to continue a conversation
>> p.58

B How to talk about a career
>> p.59

C How to talk about what happened
>> p.60

D How to talk about life stories
>> p.61

Skills Practice >> pp.62–63

Self check 10 >> p.85

11 House, home, and environment

A How to make suggestions
>> p.64

B How to say what's wrong
>> p.65

C How to compare things
>> p.66

D How to understand opinions
>> p.67

Skills Practice >> pp.68–69

Self check 11 >> p.86

12 Planning the future

A How to make an appointment
>> p.70

B How to say how you feel
>> p.71

C How to talk about future arrangements >> p.72

D How to talk about intentions
>> p.73

Skills Practice >> p.74–75

Self check 12 >> p.87

Self checks key >> pp.88–90   **Audio scripts** >> pp.91–94   **Irregular verbs** >> p.95

How to **say hello**

 Vocabulary greeting phrases

1 Match the pictures and phrases.

1 Good afternoon!   2 Good evening!   3 Good morning!

2 Complete the conversations.

What's your name again   Oops   What's your name
~~Hello~~   And you   My name's

Day 1

A ¹*Hello* _____!

B Hello! ² _____?

A My name's Bob.

B Sorry? ³ _____?

A Bob. My name's Bob. Nice to meet you!

Day 2

B Hello again, Jim.

A Hello, Jennifer. ⁴ _____ Bob.

B ⁵ _____! Hello, Bob. How are you?

A I'm fine, thanks. ⁶ _____?

B I'm fine.

3 Put the conversation in order.

- ☐ Oops! Hello, Jennifer. How are you?
- ☐ Hello, Bob! My name's Jennifer!
- ☐ I'm fine too.
- ☐ I'm fine thanks. And you?
- ☑ Hello again, Julia!

B **Pronunciation** rhythm and stress

4 **1A.1▶** Listen and tick ✓ the names you hear.

- ☐ Elaine   ☐ Drew
- ☐ Jane   ☐ Hugh
- ☐ Germaine   ☐ Stu

5 Listen again. Write the names.

A	Hello, good	**morning!**	**What's** your	**name?**
B	Hello, good	**morning!**	**My** name's	¹ _____.
A	**Nice** to	**meet** you!	**My** name's	² _____.
B	Hello,		³ _____.	**Nice** to meet **you!**

6 Listen again and practise saying the sentences.

> **And you?** Complete the conversation.
>
> A Hi! What's your name?
>
> You _____. And you?
>
> A I'm Alan. How are you?
>
> You _____
>
> A OK! See you later!
>
> You _____

How well can you say hello and ask people's names now?
Go back to the Student's Book ≫ p.7 and tick ✓ the line again.

How to say phone numbers & email addresses

G possessives *my, your, his, her*   **V** letters and numbers   **P** letters and numbers

A Pronunciation letters and numbers

1 **1B.1▶** Listen and correct the mistakes.

1 Phone numbers

Small, JC, 27 Butlin Rd............................	⁸3̶9̶46652
Smith, PA, 3 Stratford Pl.............................	0997411
Smith, RS, 91 Brisbane Ave........................	4065589
Spigott, LP, 144 Mitchell Dr........................	2213074

2 Email addresses

@	**Patty** iou20@buzby.net	**Carla** quick14@spt.com
	Tomas okchen@fanzine.	**Linda** lin3@livebird.org

3 Websites

 SHOP ONLINE

For music	▶ **www.toptunes.esl**
For medicine	▶ **www.qgetwell.co.uk**
For photos	▶ **www.digipiks.net**
For books	▶ **www.riadit.net**

B Vocabulary letters and numbers

A = 1	H = 8	O = 15	V = 22
B = 2	I = 9	P = 16	W = 23
C = 3	J = 10	Q = 17	X = 24
D = 4	K = 11	R = 18	Y = 25
E = 5	L = 12	S = 19	Z = 26
F = 6	M = 13	T = 20	
G = 7	N = 14	U = 21	

Example   13 - 25   14 - 1 - 13 - 5   9 - 19   18 - 5 - 24
            My   name   is   Rex.

2 What is the message?

7 - 15 - 15 - 4   13 - 15 - 18 - 14 - 9 - 14 - 7 !

_____ _____ !

8 - 15 - 23   1 - 18 - 5   25 - 15 - 21 ?

_____ _____ _____ ?

3 Write your own message in numbers.

C Grammar possessives *my, your, his, her*

4 Complete the conversations with these words.

my   her   his   your

1 **A** Hello! What's
     your name?
  B I'm Craig. And you?
  A _____ name's
     Gemma.
  B Nice to meet you!

2 **B** Mm! What's
     _____ name?
  A Irvina.
  B And what's

     _____

     phone number?
  A It's 77 33 74.

3 **A** Mm! What's
     _____ name?
  B Serge.
  A And what's

     _____

     phone number?
  B I don't know.

And you? Answer the questions.
What's your name?
What's your phone number?
And what's your email address?

How to give your name and address

G pronouns and possessives; present simple of *be* ⊞   V parts of an address; numbers 20+   P stress in questions

A Vocabulary numbers 20+

1 Write the answers in numbers.
1 thirteen + nine = _22_
2 forty – three = ____
3 twenty-seven + seventeen = ____
4 eighty-five – fifteen = ____
5 a hundred and six + twelve = ____
6 a hundred and thirty – sixty-five = ____
7 eleven + forty-two = ____
8 ninety-nine – ten = ____
9 a hundred – four = ____
10 sixty-seven + thirty-four = ____

2 Complete the crossword.

Across **2** 82 **5** 76 **7** 31 **8** 50 **9** 40
Down **1** 49 **3** 22 **4** 33 **6** 94

B Grammar pronouns and possessives; present simple of *be* ⊞

3 Match the pronouns with *am*, *is*, or *are*.
1 I _am = I'm_ ____
2 he _____
3 she _____
4 we _____
5 they _____

4 Complete the sentences with your answers from exercise 3 and these words.

his   her   my   our   their

1 _I'm_ from Germany.
  _____ name's Helga.

2 _____ from Poland. _____ name's Iwona.
3 _____ from Russia. _____ name's Sergei.

4 _____ from China. _____ names are Lee and Ting.
5 _____ from Canada. _____ names are Marc and Claire.

C Pronunciation stress in questions

5 Match the questions and answers.
1 ☐c **What's** your **first** name? a P-A-L-M-E-R.
2 ☐ **What's** your **sur**name? b 42 Ashford Street, Toronto.
3 ☐ **How** do you **spell** that? c ~~Claire.~~
4 ☐ **Where** are you **from**? d Palmer.
5 ☐ **What's** your ad**dress**? e Canada.

6 1C.1▶ Listen and check.

7 Listen again and copy the stress.

And you? Answer the questions from exercise 5.
1
2
3
4
5

How well can you give your name and address now?
Go back to the Student's Book ≫ p.11 and tick ✓ the line again.

How to start a conversation

G present simple of *be* ⊞ ⊟ ? V *Mr, Mrs, Ms, Miss*; polite words and phrases

A Vocabulary polite words and phrases

1 Complete the conversations with these words.

please   thanks   sorry   thank you   excuse me

1 **A** *Excuse me*, two coffees, _____.
  B Here you are.
  A _____ _____ very much!

2 **A** How are you, James?
  B I'm fine, _____. And you?

3 **A** Hello, Miss Jones.
  B It's Ms Jones!
  A Oh, _____!

4 **A** _____ I'm late!
  B That's OK, sit down.
  A _____!

5 **A** _____ _____, what's your name again?
  B Sally.
  A Hi, Sally. I'm Jake.

B Grammar present simple of *be* ⊞ ⊟ ?

2 Underline the correct words.

1 'We're / You're Coldplay. We're / You're from England.'
2 Julia Roberts is / are American. He's / She's single.
3 'Hi, my name's Jean Reno. I'm / He's not American – I'm / He's French!'
4 Ewan McGregor is from Scotland. He's / It's a country in Europe. Is / Are he single? Yes, that's right – I'm / He's single.
5 Mel Gibson and Robyn Gibson is / are single. Sorry, that's not right. We're / They're married.
6 Celine Dion am / is Canadian. She isn't / aren't single, she's / he's married.

3 Match 1–6 with a–f.

1 ☐ *d* Are you   a you from?
2 ☐ Is your   b a teacher?
3 ☐ What's   c name Ewan?
4 ☐ Where are   d ~~married?~~
5 ☐ Is your mum   e old are you?
6 ☐ How   f your phone number?

4 Match the answers with the questions in exercise 3.

a ☐ *1* No, I'm single.
b ☐ I'm 26.
c ☐ 07700 900443.
d ☐ No, my name's Ian.
e ☐ Yes, she is.
f ☐ I'm from London.

And you? Complete the conversation.

You Excuse me, _____ _____ from Germany?
B Yes, I am. And you?
You I'm from _____. What's your name?
B My name's Ulrich.
You I'm _____. _____!
B Nice to meet you! Are you married?
You _____. And you?
B No, I'm not. I'm single.
You Oh. Coffee?
B Yes, please!

How well can you start a conversation now?
Go back to the Student's Book >> p.13 and tick ✓ the line again.

7

Unit 1 Skills Practice

A Read for detail

1 Read the business cards and complete the table.

UNIVERSITY OF LENINGRAD

Ivana Kuznetsov
Department of Organic Chemistry

Ulitsa Rynok 27, Novgorod, Russia
TEL: 667 4321   EMAIL: kuznetsov@len.ac.ru

PQ OIL CORPORATION

Brian J. Wilson
Accounts Manager

- 37, Queen St, Toronto, Canada
- Tel: 0909 8790981
- Email: bjwilson@pqoil.net

Enrique Delgado | Sales Representative

c. Manzanares 16-4-A • 28017 Madrid • Spain
℻ 0191 498 0996
✎ edelgado17@spc.net

Yvonne Chanut

INTERPRETER & TRANSLATOR

Rue Bruxelles 16
69002 Lyon   *Tel:* 01632 960 0120
France   *Email:* yvchan@servling.net

Name	Country	Phone Number	Email address
			kuznetsov@len.ac.ru
	Canada		
		01632 960 0120	
Enrique Delgado			

2 Now write your own business card. Use your dictionary to check your job in English.

B Listen for key words and phrases

3 **1S.1▶** Listen and complete these forms.

1

First name _Marwan_
Surname _____
Age _____
Marital status _single_
Country _____
Home address _Marienstraat 37, Utrecht_
Telephone _623 579210_
Email _____
ID no. _NED39462H_

2

FIRST NAME
_____
SURNAME
van der Post
AGE
_29_
MARITAL STATUS
_____
COUNTRY
S. Africa

HOME ADDRESS
67, Durban St,
Pretoria
TELEPHONE
_____
EMAIL
gilvdp@saturnus.net
ID NO.
_____

3

First name _____
Surname _Collins_
Age _____
Marital status _____
Country _Ireland_
Home address _4, Cathedral St, Cork_
Telephone _202 7300_
Email _scorker@qtv.net_
ID no. _____

4 Listen again. Match the phrases with the conversations.
1 ☐ Sorry?
2 ☐ Can you just repeat that?
3 ☐ 1 How do you spell your surname?
4 ☐ Could you spell that for me?
5 ☐ Two more questions.
6 ☐ Four more questions, please.

5 Check the audio script on ≫ p.91.

C Read and check information

6 Tick ✓ the true sentences and correct the false sentences.

1 Marwan is 45.   *He's 35.*
2 He's from Utrecht, in Holland. ✓
3 His phone number is 632 579210.

4 Gillian is married.
5 Her home is in Pretoria.
6 She has no email address.

7 Sean's first name is Collins.
8 His passport number is 202 7300.
9 He's not married.
10 He's 31.

D Write personal information

7 Fill in the form with your personal details.

First name	
Surname	
Age	
Marital status	
Country	
Home address	
Telephone	
Email	
ID no.	

8 What does it say on forms in your language? Are any words the same or similar?

	in your language
First name	
Surname	
Age	
Marital status	
Country	
Home address	
Telephone	
Email	
ID no.	

E Read for detail

9 Read the letter and correct sentences 1–8.

Crown Hotel
15, Carlisle Road
Dumfries
24.7.07

Dear Helen,

Hello! How are you?

This is a photograph of me in Scotland. The other people in the picture are Yves, Sandra and Johann. They're my friends. Yves is a student here, and he's from Belgium. Sandra and Johann are also students. They're married, and they're from Germany. We are in a café having lunch. I meet new people every day – it's great!

There's no telephone in my room, but my mobile number is 07700 900 787, if you want to call. There are computers with the Internet in the hotel. My email address is gilvdp@saturnus.net.

Say hello to Tom and Tina for me!

Love,
Gillian

1 The letter is from ~~Helen~~.   *Gillian*
2 Gillian is in England.
3 Yves and Sandra are married.
4 Johann is from Belgium.
5 Gillian is in class.
6 There is a telephone in her room.
7 Sandra's mobile number is 07700 900 887.
8 There are computers in the café.

F Write an address

10 Put this address in order.
☐ Ireland
☐ 4, Cathedral St.
☐1☐ Mr S. Collins
☐ Cork

11 Write a friend's name and address.

Now try the Self check on ≫ p.76.

How to use English in the classroom

G imperatives V English in the classroom P counting syllables

A Vocabulary English in the classroom

1 Complete the words with *a, e, i, o,* or *u.*

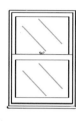

1 p e nc i l

2 p_ct_r_

3 _mbr_ll_

4 w_nd_w

5 st_d_nt

6 m_p

7 d_sk   8 ch__r   9 t__ch_r   10 b__rd

2 Read the conversations. Put the questions in order.

A Excuse me! English in what's this
  1 *What's this in English* ?
B It's a picture.
A Sorry? please that you repeat can
  2 _____ ?
B A picture.
A spell you do how that
  3 _____ ?
B P-I-C-T-U-R-E.
A Thank you!

A Open the window, please!
B slowly that can say please you
  4 _____ ?
A Open the window.
B Thank you. that write please you can
  5 _____ ?
A Yes. Look at the board.

B Grammar imperatives

3 Complete the instructions with the best word.
read write listen ~~open~~ close look ask

1 _open_____ the umbrella
2 _____ a question
3 _____ on the board
4 _____ the window
5 _____ to the CD
6 _____ at the clock
7 _____ the exercise

C Pronunciation counting syllables

4 Say the words aloud and write them in the correct box.
~~question~~ Monday afternoon underline Wednesday
umbrella answer evening English weekend
Thursday Saturday

2 syllables	3 syllables
question	

5 **2A.1▸** Listen and check.

6 Listen again and repeat.

And you? Write the instructions in your language.

Listen and check. _____
Match the words and the pictures. _____
_____
Work with a partner. _____
Underline the correct word. _____
Ask and answer. _____

How well can you use English in the classroom now?
Go back to the Student's Book >> p.17 and tick ✓ the line again.

How to introduce your family

G possessive *'s*; demonstratives *this, that, these, those* **v** family

A Vocabulary family

→→ The **Oliver** family ←←

Caroline —— Mark

Luca   Caitlin

1 Tick ✓ the true sentences and correct the false sentences.

1 Luca is Mark's father.
   Luca is Mark's son   .

2 Luca is Caitlin's sister.
   _____ .

3 Caroline is Mark's husband.
   _____ .

4 Mark is Luca's mother.
   _____ .

5 Caroline is Caitlin's mother.
   _____ .

6 Luca is Caroline's husband.
   _____ .

7 Mark is Luca and Caitlin's father.
   _____ .

8 Caitlin is Mark's son.
   _____ .

9 Caitlin and Luca are Mark and Caroline's parents.
   _____ .

B Grammar possessive *'s*; demonstratives

2 Introduce the Oliver family. Complete the sentences.

1 That's Mark. *His*____ wife*'s*_____ name*'s*_____ Caroline.

2 This is Luca. _____ sister _____ name _____ Caitlin.

3 That's Caroline. _____ children _____ names _____ Caitlin and Luca.

4 This is Caitlin. _____ father _____ name _____ Mark.

5 These two are Mark and Caroline. They _____ Caitlin and Luca _____ parents.

6 Those two are Caitlin and Luca. They _____ Mark and Caroline _____ children.

3 Complete the sentences with *this, that, these,* or *those.*

1 *That*____'s my dog.

2 _____ are my sons.

3 _____ are my parents.

4 _____ is my daughter.

5 _____'s my husband.

And you? Answer the questions.

What's your mother's name?

_____

What's your father's name?

_____

Are you married?

_____

How well can you introduce your family now?
Go back to the Student's Book >> p.19 and tick ✓ the line again.

How to describe people

G adjectives; articles *a*, *an* **V** people; jobs **P** linking words together

A Vocabulary people; jobs

1 Complete the words.

1 *g r a n d f a t h e r*
2 g _ _ _ _ m _ _ _ _ _
3 b _ _ f _ _ _ _
4 g _ _ _ f _ _ _ _
5 m _ _ _ _ _ _ c _ _ _ _ _
6 f _ _ _ _ _
7 t _ _ d _ _ _ _ _
8 o _ _ _ _ _ w _ _ _ _ _
9 f _ _ _ _ _ _ w _ _ _ _
10 f _ _ _ _ _ _ _ _ _
11 m _ _ _ _
12 a _ _ _ _ _
13 s _ _ _ _ _

B Grammar adjectives; articles *a*, *an*

2 Complete the phrases with *a* or *an*.

1 *a*_____ university student
2 _____ married couple
3 _____ doctor
4 _____ engineer
5 _____ young boy
6 _____ school teacher
7 _____ office worker

3 Complete the texts with the phrases from exercise 2.

These are friends who live in Switzerland. His name is Klaus and her name is Louise. They aren't married. She's 22 years old and she's ¹ *a university student*. He's about 30 and he's ² _____ at the local hospital.

These two are my friends from university. They're ³ _____. Their names are Annie and Paul. They have no children. He's ⁴ _____, a computer engineer, and she's ⁵ _____, a primary school teacher.

This is Françoise. She's 37 and she's divorced. She has two children: ⁶ _____ of six and a girl of sixteen. She isn't rich. She's ⁷ _____.

4 Underline the correct answers.

1 She's young woman / <u>a young woman</u>.
2 She isn't married / a married.
3 The man is a retired engineer / retired engineer.
4 He's taxi driver / a taxi driver.
5 They're a divorced couple / a couple divorced.
6 He's shop assistant / a shop assistant.
7 He isn't a rich / rich.

C Pronunciation linking words together

5 **2C.1▶** Listen and draw the linking symbol.
1 His girlfriend‿is‿an‿English teacher.
2 Her parents are designers.
3 She's an engineer.
4 The shop assistant is sixteen years old.
5 My boyfriend is a good actor.

6 Listen again and repeat.

And you? Write about your friends and family.

Example My grandparents are old. They aren't rich.

My best friend _____
My boy / girlfriend _____
My husband / wife _____
My brother / sister _____
My father _____
My mother _____

How well can you describe people now?
Go back to the Student's Book >> p.21 and tick ✓ the line again.

How to talk about the time

G prepositions of time *at, on*   V numbers and time   P stress in corrections

A Vocabulary time

1 **2D.1** Listen and tick ✓ the time you hear.

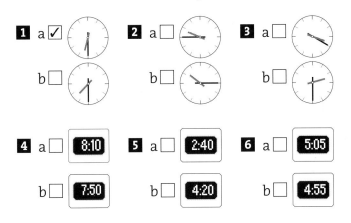

B Grammar prepositions of time *at, on*

MONDAY	
TV1	**TV2**
8.30 News	**8.45** French Class
9.00 Football Focus	**9.15** Housewife of the Day
10.30 Your Doctor	**9.45** Car Drivers

TUESDAY	
TV1	**TV2**
18.30 News	**19.00** My Family
19.30 Celebrity Singers	**19.45** News
20.30 100-question Quiz	**20.00** TV Shop

2 Write *true* or *false*.
   1 The football is on TV2.   *False*
   2 The news is on TV1 and TV2.   _____
   3 The *100-question Quiz* is on Monday evening.   _____
   4 *Housewife of the Day* is on Tuesday morning.   _____
   5 There is no news on TV2 on Monday morning.   _____
   6 *Celebrity Singers* is on TV2 at 19.30.   _____
   7 *TV Shop* is on TV2.   _____
   8 *French Class* is on TV2 at 8.45.   _____

3 Complete the sentences with *at* or *on*.
   1 *Football Focus* is on TV1 _on_ Monday _at_ 9.00.
   2 *Celebrity Singers* is on TV1 _____ Tuesday evening _____ 19.30.
   3 *French Class* is on TV2 _____ 8.45 _____ Monday.
   4 *TV Shop* is on TV2 _____ 20.00 _____ Tuesday evening.
   5 *Your Doctor* is on TV1 _____ Monday morning _____ 10.30.
   6 *My Family* is on TV2 _____ 19.00 _____ Tuesday.
   7 *Car Drivers* is _____ Tuesday _____ 9.45 on TV2.

C Pronunciation stress in corrections

4 **2D.2** Listen and underline the different information in the answer.
   1 Is it on TV1?
      No, it's on TV<u>2</u>.
   2 Is it on Monday morning?
      No, it's on Monday evening.
   3 Is it on Tuesday morning?
      No, it's on Monday morning.
   4 Is it at six o'clock?
      No, it's at twelve o'clock.
   5 Is it at ten past eight?
      No, it's at twenty past eight.
   6 Is it at five to nine?
      No, it's at five to ten.
   7 Is it the news?
      No, it's the football.

5 Listen again and copy the stress. Do you use stress like this in your language?

And you? Write the sentences in your language.

What time is it? It's half past eight.
_____

Is your class at six o'clock?
_____

It's at 11.45 on Monday morning.
_____

Unit 2 Skills Practice

A Listen for detail

1 **2S.1▶** Listen and match the messages and the places.
   a ☐ office   b ☐ school   c ☐ shop   d ☐ doctor's

2 Listen again. Write the days and times in the table.

Place	Days	Times
Doctor's	*Tuesday, Thursday*	
Office		
Shop		
School		

3 Listen again and complete the information.

   Doctor Watson's office ___*is*___ _____ _____

   the moment. The doctor is available on Tuesday

   _____ _____ _____ , from ...

4 Check the audio script on ≫ p.91.

B Listen for key words

5 **2S.2▶** Listen to Eric and number the pictures.

6 Listen again. Match the phrases with the names.
   1 ☐*d* ☐ Eric   a a shop assistant
   2 ☐ ☐ Maria   b I'm a designer
   3 ☐ ☐ Annie & Paul   c she isn't rich
   4 ☐ ☐ Françoise   d ~~25 years old~~
   5 ☐ ☐ Klaus & Louise   e they aren't married
                           f primary school teacher
                           g not my wife
                           h these are friends
                           i a married couple
                           j she's divorced

7 Check the audio script on ≫ p.91.

C Read and understand

8 Read Ana's email. Put the pictures in order.

Dear Linda,

I like my new class a lot! I study with Satomi, Pablo, and Paula. Our teacher's name is Jim. We look at the pictures in the book and Jim tells us the words. Next, we repeat the words together. Then we listen to conversations on the CD. We have a conversation with our partner, and Jim listens. He tells us if we are right or wrong. It's fun to work with a partner! Sometimes we read texts from the book and write answers to the questions. If we don't understand, we ask the teacher questions, and he helps us. Do you remember our classes at school? These classes are different!

Love,

Ana

D Write a message of introduction

9 Do you know these famous people? Match 1–4 with the pictures.

1 This is Anastacia. She's an American singer. She's 32 years old and _____.

2 This is Sade. She's an English singer and she's 47 years old. Her father's from Nigeria. She's divorced and _____. Her daughter's name is Ila.

3 This is Ronaldinho. He's a Brazilian footballer and he's 26 years old. His girlfriend is a model – _____ _____ – and they have a young son: João.

4 This is Ben Stiller and his wife. He's 40 and he's an American actor. His wife's name is Christine. She's an actress, and _____.

10 Put these phrases in the gaps in exercise 9.

her name is Janaina
they have two children
she has a daughter
she's single

11 Order the words to make sentences about Stella McCartney. Remember full stops (.) and CAPITAL letters.

1 this   stella mccartney   is
2 she's   designer   english   an
3 her   a   father   singer   is
4 she's 33   she's   years   married   old   and
5 her   is   alasdhair   name   husband's
6 they   son   have   a   baby

This is Stella McCartney. She's _____
_____
_____
_____
_____
_____
_____
_____
_____
_____
_____
_____

12 Think of ten jobs famous people do (singer, actor, etc.). Write them in your language, and write the English translation. Use your dictionary.

cantante *smf* singer

Dizionario Oxford Study per studenti d'inglese

13 Write six sentences about a famous person from your country.

This is _____.
He's / She's _____
_____
_____
_____
_____
_____
_____
_____

14 Check your writing for full stops and capital letters.

Now try the Self check on » p.77.

How to ask for information

v places **P** word stress

A Vocabulary places

1 Find the places in the puzzle.

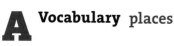

T	P	R	T	O	S	U	C	E	A	C
I	L	E	X	I	T	R	H	A	I	H
C	A	S	H	M	A	C	H	I	N	E
K	T	T	I	A	T	A	X	I	O	M
E	F	A	B	O	I	R	S	T	B	I
T	O	U	O	I	O	P	T	B	U	S
O	R	R	O	O	N	A	S	R	T	T
F	M	A	K	T	I	R	T	E	R	S
F	X	N	S	S	O	K	B	X	A	B
I	C	T	H	O	A	H	A	I	I	C
C	X	T	O	I	L	E	T	S	N	F
E	S	H	P	U	B	U	A	T	R	A

2 Complete the sentences with a place from exercise 1.
1 The train is on *platform* 5.
2 Get your tickets from the _____ _____.
3 Have dinner in a _____.
4 Get a book at a _____.
5 Park your car in a _____ _____.
6 Have a drink in a _____.

3 Read the conversations. Put the words in order.
A Excuse me!
B Yes?
A are please the where toilets
 ¹ *Where are the toilets, please* ?
B Toilets?
A Yes!
B I upstairs they're think
 ² _____.
A Thank you!

A Excuse me. platform is near 5 here
 ³ _____?
B 5 is platform this
 ⁴ _____!
A Ah, thank you!

A Excuse me. Manchester this to the is bus
 ⁵ _____?
B No, it isn't. It's near the café.
A café the where's
 ⁶ _____?
B It's over there.
A Thank you!

B Pronunciation word stress

4 **3A.1▶** Listen and write these words in the gaps.
 chemist's bookshop ~~Manchester~~
 telephones platform car park exit
 café music shop cash machines
1 Is this the train to *Manchester* ?
 No, that train's on _____ 4.
2 Excuse me! Where are the _____?
 They're over there, near the _____.
3 Where's the _____, please?
 It's upstairs, near the _____.
4 Excuse me, is this the _____?
 No, it isn't. It's over there, near the _____.
5 Excuse me, where are the _____, please?
 They're near the _____.

5 Listen again. Write the words in the correct box.

●●	●●●
platform	*Manchester*

How well can you ask for information about places now?
Go back to the Student's Book >> p.27 and tick ✓ the line again.

How to **talk about countries**

G articles *a, an, the*   **V** countries, nationalities, languages   **P** word stress

A Vocabulary countries, nationalities, languages

1 Match the countries with the flags.

1 [*d*] India   4 ☐ Canada   7 ☐ South Africa
2 ☐ Japan   5 ☐ Peru   8 ☐ Turkey
3 ☐ Spain   6 ☐ China   9 ☐ Brazil

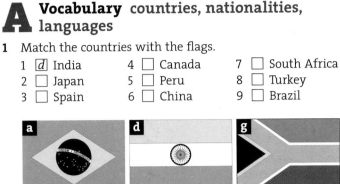

2 Write the nationalities of the countries in exercise 1.
Use your dictionary.

-n	-ian	-ish	-ese
Indian			

B Grammar articles *a, an, the*

3 Match 1–5 with a–e.

1 [*d*] Hindi is an
2 ☐ New Delhi is the
3 ☐ Chennai is a
4 ☐ The rupee is the
5 ☐ India is a

a city in India.
b country in South Asia.
c capital of India.
d ~~Indian language~~.
e currency of India.

4 Underline the correct word.

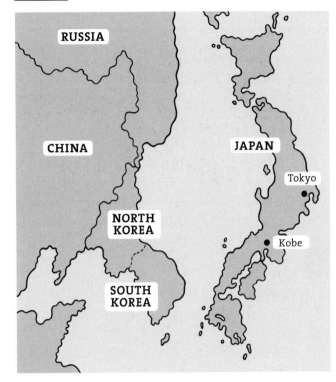

1 Tokyo is a / <u>the</u> capital of Japan.
2 Japanese is a / the language of Japan.
3 China is a / the country near Japan.
4 Kobe is a / the city near Osaka.
5 Japan is a / the country in Asia.
6 Japan is an / the island.

C Pronunciation word stress

5 Listen and write these words in the correct box.
~~Portugal~~ Portuguese Egypt Egyptian
Japan Japanese China Chinese

●•	•●	●••	•●•	••●
		Portugal		

6 **3B.1▶** Listen again and repeat.

How to say where you are in town

G plurals   **V** things and places in town   **P** plural endings

A Vocabulary things and places in town

1 Write these words in the correct box.

~~taxi~~ ~~woman~~ ~~house~~ church street children
supermarket lorry factory bus waiter
bike worker restaurant office driver school

places	people	transport
house	woman	taxi

2 Write five more words in the boxes. Use your dictionary.

B Grammar plurals

3 Write the plurals for these words.

1 city _____cities_____   5 currency _____
2 country _____   6 office _____
3 language _____   7 man _____
4 cinema _____   8 woman _____

4 Write the plurals in the phrases.

1 (driver) _drivers_ in their (car) _cars_
2 (person) _____ in (shop) _____
3 (family) _____ in (cinema) _____
4 (worker) _____ in (factory) _____
5 (child) _____ in (church) _____

5 Match the signs with the people in exercise 4.

a [ ]   b [ ]   c [1]

d [ ]   e [ ]

6 Complete the phrases with *in* or *on*.

1 _on_ his bike   5 ____ the park

2 ____ a car   6 ____ the bus

3 ____ the table   7 ____ France

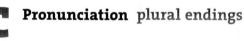

4 ____ class   8 ____ the platform

C Pronunciation plural endings

7 **3C.1▶** Listen to the singular and the plural. Write *A* or *B*.

A plural has 1 syllable	B plural has an extra syllable
car cars	page pages

1 [B] house houses   6 [ ] glass glasses
2 [ ] school schools   7 [ ] street streets
3 [ ] watch watches   8 [ ] girl girls
4 [ ] shop shops   9 [ ] town towns
5 [ ] church churches

8 Listen again and repeat.

And you? Write the names of two places in your town.

1 Two restaurants: _____
2 Two shops: _____
3 Two schools: _____

 **3C**

How well can you say where you are in town now?
Go back to the Student's Book ≫ p.31 and tick ✓ the line again.

How to talk about language skills

G present simple ⊕⊖? *do, don't* V phrases describing language ability P *Sue* /s/ or *shoe* /ʃ/

A Grammar present simple ⊕-? *do, don't*

1 Complete the conversation with *do* or *don't*.

A ¹ *Do* you speak English?

B No, I ²_____.

A ³_____ you understand English?

B Yes, I ⁴_____. I understand a little.

A ⁵_____ you read English?

B No, I ⁶_____.

A ⁷_____ you write English?

B Yes, I ⁸_____. I write a little.

A ⁹_____ you like English?

B I ¹⁰_____ know!

B Vocabulary phrases describing language ability

2 Jon is a student in a Chinese class. <u>Underline</u> the correct words.

1 I read <u>Chinese quite well</u>/quite well Chinese.

2 I write a little Chinese/Chinese a little.

3 I understand very well Chinese/Chinese very well.

4 I don't speak Chinese very well/very well Chinese.

5 I pronounce quite well Chinese/Chinese quite well.

6 I know a little vocabulary/vocabulary a little.

3 Chen and Jun are students in a German class. Write their sentences.

1 read / quite well

   *We read German quite well*_____.

2 write / not very well

   _____

3 understand / very well

   _____

4 speak / a little

   _____.

5 pronounce / not very well

   _____.

C Pronunciation *Sue* /s/ or *shoe* /ʃ/

4 Is the <u>underlined</u> sound /s/ or /ʃ/? Say these words aloud and write them in the correct box.

Rus<u>s</u>ian France <u>Sp̶a̶n̶i̶s̶h̶</u> South African Swedi<u>sh</u>
Swahili na<u>ti</u>onality currency Egyptian Poli<u>sh</u>

/s/	/ʃ/
Spanish	*Spanish*

5 Check your answers in your dictionary. Practise saying the words.

And you? Write three sentences about your English.
Example I speak English quite well.

Unit 3 Skills Practice

A Listen for key information

1 **3S.1▶** Listen to five conversations. Tick ✓ the places you hear.

☐ toilets ☐ chemist's ☐ South Street exit
☐ bus stop ☐ café ☐ cash machines

2 Listen again and write the places in the gaps.

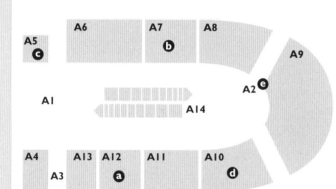

Back Street Shopping Centre

A1	car park exit	A8	4_____
A2	1_____	A9	supermarket
A3	emergency exit	A10	café
A4	taxis	A11	music shop
A5	2_____	A12	pub
A6	bookshop	A13	public phones
A7	3_____	A14	5_____

OPENING HOURS Monday–Saturday: 9.00 a.m.–6.00 p.m.
Sunday: 10.00 a.m.–5.00 p.m.

3 Listen again. Put the words in order.

1 a here is stop there bus near
*Is there a bus stop near here*_____ ?

2 the look cash machines there are
_____ .

3 I have me don't my with glasses
_____ .

4 shopping at centre other of the end the
_____ .

5 it oh is yes here
_____ !

4 Check the audio script on >> p.91.

B Read and understand messages

5 Is the information correct? Look at the map and write *true* or *false*.

1 The taxis are near the South Street exit.   *False*_____

2 The taxis are near the bookshop.   _____

3 The toilets are near the chemist's.   _____

4 There are phones in the supermarket.   _____

5 The pub is near the music shop.   _____

6 There are no cash machines at the
car park exit.   _____

7 On Tuesdays, the centre is closed.   _____

8 The centre is open on Sundays.   _____

6 Where are they? Match the text messages with the letters a–e on the map.

1 *c*
I'm at the bus stop in the street.

2 ☐
I'm in the pub, near the public phones.

3 ☐
I'm at the chemist's, near the toilets.

4 ☐
We're at the South Street exit, near the supermarket.

5 ☐
I'm in the café, near the music shop.

C Read for key information

7 Match the hotels and the guests.

1 A family with three young children and a dog. They travel by train.
2 A middle-aged couple. They are in a car, and want to walk around the city.
3 A young couple. The want to go out in the evening and dance.

a

- Large car park
- Near city centre and museums
- 3 restaurants – Chinese, Indian, and American
- Bar
- Cable TV
- No pets

b

- Five-minute walk to station
- Swimming pool
- Family rooms
- TV and telephone in every room
- No smoking
- Pets welcome

c

- Car park
- Near pubs, nightclubs, and cinema
- Restaurant
- Cable TV
- Bar

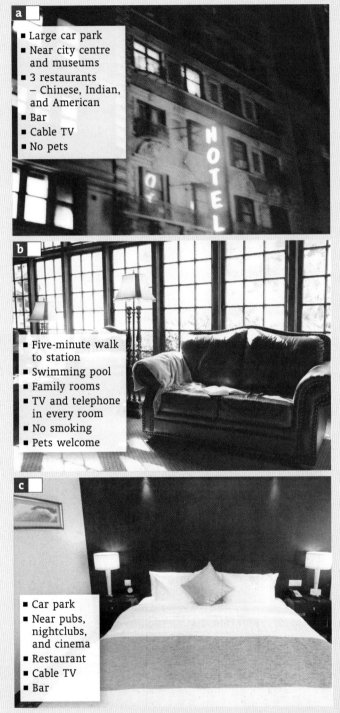

8 <u>Underline</u> three or four words you don't know. Use your dictionary to look up their meaning.

D Write quiz questions

9 Make a list of ten countries. Write the nationalities. Use your dictionary.

country	nationality
Scotland	Scottish

10 Complete the text with these words.

what's   currency   nationality   ~~flag~~   language

This is the Scottish ¹ *flag*_____. The ²_____
of Scotland is the pound. The ³_____ is
English and the ⁴_____ is Scottish.
But ⁵_____ the capital of Scotland?

a London   b Cardiff   c Edinburgh

11 Correct the text. Add CAPITAL letters.

This is the argentinian flag. the capital of argentina is buenos aires and the language is spanish. but what's the currency of argentina?

a euro   b peso   c dollar

12 Write a quiz question about another country. Write three or four sentences.

This is the _____ flag. _____
_____
_____
_____

13 Check your sentences for capital letters.

Now try the Self check on >> p.78.

How to **respond to news**

G prepositions of place *at*   **V** signs; responses to news   **P** responses to news

A Vocabulary signs

1 Find the eleven signs and write them below.

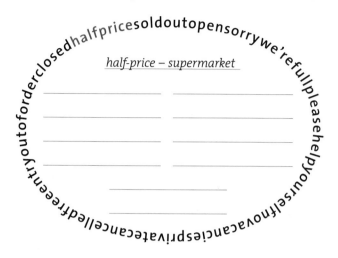

outofordercloseedhalfpricesoldoutopensorrywe'refullpleasehelpyourselfnovacanciesprivatecancelledfreeentry

half-price – supermarket

_____   _____

_____   _____

_____   _____

_____

_____   _____

_____

2 Where can you see the signs? Write a different place for each sign.

3 Complete the sentences with some of the signs from exercise 1.

1 A Do you have a room for tonight, please?
   B I'm sorry, we have _no vacancies_ for tonight.

2 A Is it €5 for the cinema tomorrow night?
   B No, €2.50! It's _____ on Sunday nights!

3 Flight BD332 is _____ because of bad weather.

4 A Do you have your ticket?
   B No, the machine is _____ _____ _____!

5 I'm sorry, the office is _____ now.
   We are _____ on Monday at nine o'clock.

6 A Is that the toilet?
   B No, the sign on the door says '_____
   – no entry'.

B Vocabulary responses to news

4 Match 1–10 with a–j.
   1 [c] The football's on in five minutes but
   2 ☐ I'm at the supermarket and
   3 ☐ My car! My car!
   4 ☐ We have a
   5 ☐ My sister has
   6 ☐ We get married
   7 ☐ My father's
   8 ☐ My cat
   9 ☐ School is
   10 ☐ It's 9.30

   a everything is half-price today. I'm sorry! / That's great!
   b new car! Oh no! / Oh really?
   c ~~the TV is out of order~~. Good luck! / Oh no!
   d It's not in the car park! Oh no! / Good luck!
   e a new baby. That's great! / I'm sorry!
   f and my exam's at ten o'clock. Good luck! / Well done!
   g on Monday! I'm sorry! / Good luck!
   h closed today. Well done! / That's great!
   i isn't very well. That's great! / I'm sorry!
   j in bed. Oh really? / Well done!

5 For the news in exercise 4, <u>underline</u> the best response.

C Pronunciation responses to news

6 **4A.1▶** Listen and check your answers. Copy the pronunciation of the responses.

And you? Write your good news and your bad news.
1
2
3
4

How well can you respond to good and bad news now?
Go back to the Student's Book >> p.37 and tick ✓ the line again.

How to say dates

G prepositions of time *at, in, on*   **V** months and ordinal numbers   **P** /θ/

A   Vocabulary months and ordinal numbers

1 Follow the instructions and complete the puzzle.
   1 Write the last letter of the first month.
   2 Write the third letter of the third month.
   3 Write the first letter of the fourth month.
   4 Write the second letter of the seventh month.
   5 Write the last letter of the ninth month.
   6 Write the sixth letter of the twelfth month.
   7 Write the fourth letter of the sixth month.
   8 Write the first letter of the second month.

   Y

   ↑

   9 Find the month in the letters. _____

B   Pronunciation /θ/

2 **4B.1▶** Listen and write the dates.
   1 *the seventh of April*   4 _____
   2 _____   5 _____
   3 _____   6 _____

3 Listen again and repeat. Practise the /θ/ sound.

C   Grammar prepositions of time *at, in, on*

May

19	
20	
21	1.15 Dentist
22	
23	
24	Doctor 9.30
25	
26	
27	Theatre 20.30
28	
29	
30	
31	21.00 Cinema

June

1	
2	
3	Party! 20.00
4	
5	Train to Berlin 22.00
6	
7	
8	Birthday – restaurant 19.30
9	
10	16.30 German exam
11	

4 Complete the sentences with *at, in,* or *on*.
   1 When's the cinema?   It's _on_ May 31st _at_ 9 p.m.
   2 And the theatre?   That's ____ May 27th ____ 8.30 ____ the evening.
   3 When's the restaurant?   That's ____ June, ____ the 8th, ____ 7.30 p.m.
   4 And the doctor?   It's ____ 9.30 ____ May 24th.
   5 And the dentist?   It's ____ May 21st ____ 1.15.
   6 Oh, and my German exam?   It's ____ 4.30 ____ the afternoon ____ June 10th.
   7 And the train to Berlin?   That's ____ June, ____ the 5th, ____ 10 p.m.
   8 When's the party?   It's ____ 8 p.m. ____ June 3rd.

5 Order the words to make questions.
   A birthday is your date what
   1 _____?
   B It's on February 12th.
   A time English what your class is
   2 _____?
   B It's at 10.30.
   A shopping day you what go do
   3 _____?
   B On Fridays.
   A holidays your when are summer
   4 _____?
   B They're in August.

And you? Answer the questions in exercise 5.
1
2
3
4

How to describe habits

G present simple with *he / she / it*   V morning habits   P final *-s*

A Vocabulary morning habits

1 Write these phrases in the correct box.

~~to work~~   breakfast   back to bed   up   for a run
to the kitchen   a shower   dressed   tea or coffee

go	get	have
to work		

B Grammar present simple with *he / she / it*

2 Read the text and put the pictures in order.

Tom ¹ *is* a bit different. He works in a factory, not in an office, and he works at night. He ²_____ work at nine in the evening and ³_____ at five in the morning. When he gets home, he ⁴_____ a shower and ⁵_____ to bed. At about eleven o'clock, he gets up and has breakfast: coffee and toast. After breakfast he ⁶_____ the newspaper or ⁷_____ to the news on the radio. Then he ⁸_____ tennis with friends, or sometimes he ⁹_____ languages. His new language is Italian – it's his third foreign language. At the weekend he gets up late and ¹⁰_____ TV.

3 Complete the text with these verbs in the correct form.

~~be~~ go watch finish study play have
read start listen

4 Write the complete questions.

1 Where / work *Where does he work*_____? In a factory.

2 When / finish work _____?
At five in the morning.

3 What time / get up _____?
About eleven o'clock.

4 What / have for breakfast _____?
Coffee and toast.

5 What / do after breakfast _____?
He reads the newspaper.

6 play football _____? No, he doesn't.

7 When / get up late _____?
At the weekend.

C Pronunciation final *-s*

5 Complete the lines with these words and phrases.

TV   the house   late   for a run   the mail
her teeth   ~~early~~   work   fruit for breakfast

1 He wakes up   *early*_____

2 She gets up   _____

3 He checks   _____

4 She goes   _____

5 He has   _____

6 She leaves   _____

7 He watches   _____

8 She brushes   _____

9 He finishes   _____

6 **4C.1▶** Listen and check.

7 Listen again and repeat. Copy the pronunciation.

> **And you?** Answer the questions.
>
> Where do you work / study?
> _____
>
> What time do you get up in the morning?
> _____
>
> Do you have a big breakfast?
> _____
>
> When do you leave home?
> _____

How well can you describe morning habits now?
Go back to the Student's Book >> p.41 and tick ✓ the line again.

How to describe a typical day

G adverbs of frequency   **P** *leave* /iː/ or *live* /ɪ/

A   Grammar   adverbs of frequency

1 Match the two parts of the actions.

late for work   a coffee break   the boss   the clock
~~to work~~   home   the newspaper   some letters   lunch

1 drive *to work*   2 arrive _____   3 read _____

4 have _____   5 write _____   6 have _____

7 listen to _____   8 look at _____   9 drive _____

2 Write the sentences with the adverbs in brackets.

1 He drives to work. (always) *He always drives to work.*

2 He arrives early for work. (not often)
   He doesn't often arrive early for work .

3 He reads the newspaper. (often)
   _____ .

4 He's late for his coffee break. (never)
   _____ .

5 He writes letters. (sometimes)
   _____ .

6 He has lunch for two hours. (often)
   _____ .

7 He listens to the boss. (not usually)
   _____ .

8 He looks at the clock. (always)
   _____ .

9 He's the first to leave work. (always)
   _____ .

3 Order the words to make questions.

A job like your you do
   1 *Do you like your job* _____ ?
B It's OK.
A when holiday you on go do
   2 _____ ?
B Usually in August, sometimes in December.
A usually you go do where
   3 _____ ?
B To the beach or to another country.
A friends family with you or go do
   4 _____ ?
B With friends.
A holiday car the you do on use
   5 _____ ?
B Yes, always.

B   Pronunciation   *leave* /iː/ or *live* /ɪ/

4 **4D.1▶** Say these words aloud and write them in the correct box.

~~this~~ mean sleep people listen finish repeat
thing three

leave /iː/	live /ɪ/
	this

5 Check your answers in your dictionary. Practise saying the words.

And you? Answer the questions in exercise 3.	
1	
2	
3	
4	
5	

How well can you describe a typical day now?
Go back to the Student's Book ≫ p.43 and tick ✓ the line again.

Unit 4 Skills Practice

A Read and understand

1 Match the pictures with the paragraphs.

a Selina is a ten-year-old girl who lives with her brothers and sisters, her parents, grandmother, and uncle and aunt. The family live in a small village in Ethiopia and they have breakfast together early in the morning, at about six o'clock.

b At seven o'clock, after breakfast, the adults leave the village. The men work in the fields, and the women get water and firewood.

c Selina and one of her sisters clean the house, wash the dishes, and take the small children to another aunt's house.

d At eight o'clock, Selina goes to school. She is the only person in the family who goes to school. The children often have classes outside, in the shade of a big tree.

e At half-past twelve, the children go home to have lunch. Selina usually has an hour to do her homework before she goes back to school in the afternoon. Afternoon classes are from half-past two to five.

f The family come back home after work late in the afternoon, about half-past six. They have dinner near the fire. After dinner, the small children often play together, the schoolchildren do their homework and the adults have conversations with their friends. They usually go to bed at about half-past nine.

2 <u>Underline</u> three or four words you don't know. Guess their meaning, and then check in your dictionary.

B Listen for key words

3 **4S.1▶** Listen and <u>underline</u> the countries you hear.

Austria
England
France
Germany
Holland
Italy
Poland

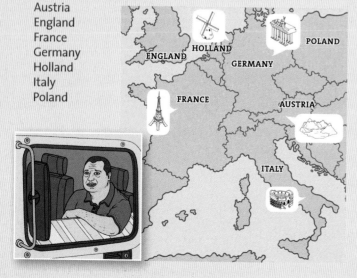

4 Listen and match the days and the countries.

1	d	Monday	a	Italy
2	☐	Tuesday	b	Germany
3	☐	Wednesday	c	France
4	☐	Thursday	d	Holland
5	☐	Friday	e	Austria
6	☐	Saturday and Sunday		

5 Listen to the beginning of the interview again. Complete the text.

A So, Jack, you're a lorry driver. Tell me *about* _____ normal week.

J Normal week? _____ _____ _____ any normal weeks! Yeah, well, I usually work _____ _____ _____, but, erm, it's often _____ too.

6 Check the audio script on >> p.92.

C Read for detail

7 Read Ana's email and complete the table.

Hello Giselle!

How are you? I'm really looking forward to your visit. I'm very busy, so I don't have much time to see you. I work three mornings a week from eight till two, that's Monday, Wednesday, and Friday, and the other two days I work in the afternoon and evening, from three till nine o'clock. I always have lunch at two o'clock, even on Saturdays. I normally go shopping on Thursday mornings. On Monday and Friday afternoons I often go to the gym to get some exercise, usually at about five o'clock. Oh, and I have my French class on Tuesday mornings. In the evenings I like to stay at home, but on Friday and Saturday evenings I go out with my friends. And Saturday is my day for getting up late. I have breakfast about half-past ten on Saturday mornings. Maybe Sunday is the best day to come!

Write back soon!

Love,

Ana

Monday	8.00–2.00 work	2.00 lunch	5.00 _____
Tuesday	9.00–11.00 _____	2.00 _____	3.00–9.00 _____
Wednesday	8.00–2.00 work	2.00 _____	
Thursday	9.30–11.30 _____	2.00 lunch	3.00–9.00 _____
Friday	8.00–2.00 work	2.00 lunch	5.00 _____ evening
Saturday	10.30 _____	2.00 _____	evening

8 Write *true* or *false*.

1 Ana doesn't work at the weekend.   *True*

2 She doesn't have lunch on Tuesdays.   _____

3 She goes shopping one day a week.   _____

4 She goes to the gym on Mondays.   _____

5 She studies French on Tuesdays.   _____

6 She goes out every night.   _____

7 On Saturday mornings she has breakfast very early. _____

D Write about your day

9 Read part of Giselle's email. Find and correct eight more spelling mistakes.

     usually

...I ~~ussually~~ go shoping on

Teusdays, when most poeple

are at work. My favourite day

is Wensday too. That's when I

often go out on my byke. Two

days a week I go to a driving

school. My fahter can't drive

now, so I have driving lesons

to help my famly...

10 Complete the sentences about your day.

I always _____

_____ .

I often _____

_____ .

I don't often _____

_____ .

I usually _____

_____ .

I sometimes _____

_____ .

I never _____

_____ .

11 Check your writing for spelling mistakes.

Now try the Self check on >> p.79.

How to introduce people

G object pronouns; prepositions of place *next to, opposite*   **V** phrases to introduce people   **P** vowels

A Vocabulary phrases to introduce people

1 Order the words to make sentences and questions.

1 me you remember do   *Do you remember me*   ?
2 boyfriend know my you do

_____ ?

3 what's again sorry name your

_____ ?

4 I'm sorry but your name don't I remember

_____ .

5 and them meet come

_____

B Grammar object pronouns

2 Complete the sentences with these words.

~~you~~ us them it him her me

1 I know *you*, but you don't know _____ .

2 She likes _____ , but he doesn't like _____ .

3 We know _____ , but they don't know _____ .

4 The dog likes the children, but they don't like _____ .

3 Complete the conversation about the people in the picture.

Bill   Who's that? I don't know ¹ *him* .
Maggie   That's Dick. ² _____ works in my office. He sits next to me.
B   And who's that woman next to ³ _____ ? I don't know ⁴ _____ .
M   That's Maya. I think she's Dick's girlfriend.
B   And that couple over there? Who are ⁵ _____ ?
M   Don't ask ⁶ _____ ! I don't know ⁷ _____ !
B   Look! There's Cathy.
M   I don't remember ⁸ _____ .
B   Don't you? ⁹ _____ lives near us, opposite the newspaper shop.
M   Oh, yes.
B   Coffee?
M   No, thanks. I don't really like ¹⁰ _____ .

C Pronunciation vowels *a, e, i, o, u*

4 Match the vowel with the pronunciation. Use your dictionary.

~~a~~ e i o u

/əʊ/ ____   /iː/ ____   /eɪ/ *a*   /aɪ/ ____   /juː/ ____

5 Which words have the same vowel sound? Match the words with the letter.

~~day~~ ~~tea~~ ~~buy~~ ~~go~~ ~~you~~ rule three know two five blue eight nine speak school drive say play name show like meet

a *day* _____
e *tea* _____
i *buy* _____
o *go* _____
u *you* _____

6 Check your answers in your dictionary.

How well can you introduce people now?
Go back to the Student's Book >> p.47 and tick ✓ the line again.

How to **describe people and objects**

G order of adjectives   **V** adjectives   **P** *man* /æ/ or *men* /e/

A Vocabulary adjectives

1 Write the opposites.

1

fat cat   *thin cat*

2

black cat _____

3

old bike _____

4

big bike _____

5

tall tree _____

6

old clock _____

7

long street _____

8

fat book _____

9

short hair _____

B Grammar order of adjectives

2 Put the words in the correct order.

1	taxi	a	black	big
2	old	buses	grey	two
3	grey	offices	tall	
4	big	a	factory	new
5	tall	four	trees	green
6	bike	a	white	new
7	fat	two	cats	white
8	man	a	blond	short
9	a	black	umbrella	big

a big black taxi
_____
_____
_____
_____
_____
_____
_____
_____

3 Match the phrases in exercise 2 with the things in the picture.

C Pronunciation *man* /æ/ or *men* /e/

4 Say these words aloud and write them in the correct box.

~~get~~ ~~bag~~ have cat spell bank text guess
fact very friend bad <u>again</u>

/æ/ **man**	/e/ **men**
bag	*get*

5 Check your answers in your dictionary. Practise saying the words.

And you? Complete the sentences.

In my home, I've got a new _____ and a big _____. I've also got
an old _____, a black _____ and a white _____. I haven't
got a fat _____ or a tall _____.

How well can you describe people and objects now?
Go back to the Student's Book ≫ p.49 and tick ✓ the line again.

29

How to ask for things in shops

G *have got*   **V** office supplies; shopping phrases

A Vocabulary office supplies

1 Complete the crossword.

Across

3

5

6

9

Down

1

2

4

7

8

B Grammar *I / you / we / they have got*

2 Complete the sentences with the correct form of *have*.

1 We'_ve__ got two sons, but we _____ got a daughter.

2 _____ you got a car?
No, I _____ .

3 _____ they got any children?
Yes, they _____ . They'_____ got a daughter.

4 I'_____ got a computer, but I _____ got a printer.

3 Put the words in order to make the questions and answers.

1 car you a got have
Have you got a car _____?
No, motorbike a got I've
_____.

2 children any got you have
_____?
Yes, two boy girls got and we've a
_____.

3 got any they pets have
_____?
Yes, a two got cats they've and mouse
_____.

C Vocabulary shopping phrases

4 Match the questions and answers.

1 [c] Have you got any colour ink?
2 [ ] Excuse me, can you help me?
3 [ ] Black or colour?
4 [ ] Anything else?
5 [ ] How much is that?

a That's all, thanks.
b Twenty-seven euros.
c ~~No, I'm sorry, we haven't.~~
d Colour, please.
e Yes, of course.

And you? Write these phrases in your language.

Can I help you? _____?

Here you are. _____.

That's all, thanks. _____.

How well can you ask for things in a shop now?
Go back to the Student's Book ≫ p.51 and tick ✓ the line again.

How to ask about people's interests

G *has got* V gifts P stress timing

 A **Grammar** *he / she / it has got*

1 Match the questions and answers.
1 *d* Have you got a watch?
2 ☐ What has she got in her bag?
3 ☐ Has the hotel got a car park?
4 ☐ Does she cook?
5 ☐ Has he got any pets?
6 ☐ What colour eyes has he got?
7 ☐ Does he like animals?
8 ☐ Has she got a car?

a A pen, a pencil, and a notebook.
b Yes, he has. A dog.
c Sometimes!
d ~~Yes, I have~~.
e Blue.
f I'm sorry, it hasn't.
g No, she doesn't drive.
h Yes, he does.

2 Look at the pictures and write ten differences.
1 *She's got an old computer but he's got a new one* .
2 _____ .
3 _____ .
4 _____ .
5 _____ .
6 _____ .
7 _____ .
8 _____ .
9 _____ .
10 _____ .

B **Pronunciation** stress timing

3 Complete the sentences with these words.
nice ~~car~~ house dog watch

1 I've **got** a **bike** but I   **ha**ven't got a *car* .
2 I've **got** a **clock** but I   **want** to get a _____ .
3 I've **got** a **cat** but I'd   **ra**ther have a _____ .
4 I've **got** a **flat** but I   **want** to buy a _____ .
5 I've **got** a **wife** but she **isn't** very _____ .
   Sorry, dear.

4 **5D.1**▶ Listen and check. Copy the stress.

And you? Describe your room.
Example My room's got a bed, a cupboard, and two chairs.
My room _____ . It hasn't got _____ . It's got _____ _____ and _____ .

Unit 5 Skills Practice

A Read and understand

1 Read the puzzle and complete the chart.

The Smith family live at Number 1, and they've got two children. The family in the house opposite them have one teenage child. This teenager hasn't got any pets. Her boyfriend lives at Number 5.

The Jones family live at the other end of the street, at Number 6. They haven't got any children, but they've got pets: two cats and a dog. The Molina family live next to the Joneses. They've got two children, who play with the three children in the house opposite. The Molina children also play with their pet rabbit.

The Patel family live next to the Smiths. They've got two dogs. The dogs don't like the Smiths' grey cat. The Kowalski family live opposite the Joneses. They've got one teenage child and three cats.

The family opposite the Smiths are the Dixons, and they've got a big black car. Their neighbours at Number 4 have got a big grey car, but the neighbours at Number 6 haven't got a car. They've got a motorbike. The boy in the house opposite would like to ride that motorbike. His parents have got an old blue car.

The family opposite the Molinas have got two cars, one for the husband and one for the wife. Their neighbours at Number 1 have got a red car.

Nº 1
family _Smith_
children _____
transport _____
pets _____

Nº 3
family _____
children _____
transport _____
pets _____

Nº 5
family _____
children _1 boy_
transport _____
pets _____

Nº 2
family _____
children _____
transport _black car_
pets _____

Nº 4
family _____
children _____
transport _____
pets _rabbit_

Nº 6
family _Jones_
children _____
transport _____
pets _____

B Listen for key phrases

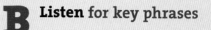

2 **5S.1▶** Listen to people meeting. Tick ✓ the number of speakers.
  a ☐ 1 ☐ 2 ☐ 3 ☐ 4
  b ☐ 1 ☐ 2 ☐ 3 ☐ 4
  c ☐ 1 ☐ 2 ☐ 3 ☐ 4

3 Match the conversations with the people.
  ☐ Jenny meets Ricardo and Elena.
  ☐ Stella meets Sheila.
  ☐ Henry meets Mr Patel.

4 Listen again. Match the conversations with the phrases.
  1 ☐ Come and meet her.
  2 ☐ Come and meet him.
  3 ☐ Do you remember me?
  4 ☐ This is my wife.
  5 ☐a Do you know my brother?
  6 ☐ Sorry, what's your name again?

5 Read and listen to the first conversation again. Correct five more mistakes.
                          How
  A Mr Patel! ~~Who~~ are you?

  B Fine, thanks, Mike. And you?

  A I'm fine, thank you. Do you know my brother Henry?

  B No, I don't think so.

  A Come and meet her. Henry, this is Mr Patel, your neighbour. Mr Patel, Henry, my father.

  C Nice to meet you!

  B Yes, me too.

6 Check the audio script on ≫ p.92.

C Read for detail

7 Match the descriptions and the pictures.

1 She's got big blue eyes and short brown hair. She lives in the flat next door and she works in the local hairdresser's. She often goes to an Indian restaurant, and she likes green tea. She's got a little brown dog that she takes for a walk every afternoon. She reads fashion magazines and listens to techno music at the weekend.

2 She's got blue eyes and short hair. She works in the hairdresser's and likes Chinese food, but she doesn't go out very often. She listens to pop music and reads the newspaper every day. She's got a big dog, and she takes it to the park every morning.

3 She's got brown eyes and long blond hair. She lives in the flat next door and she's a student at the local university. She doesn't like dogs, but she's got a small white cat called Boris. She usually buys a newspaper and reads it in a café with a cup of coffee.

a

b

c

8 Find these words in the texts.

1 a word that means *Saturday and Sunday*   weekend

2 the opposite of *short*   _____

3 a word that means the same as *small*   _____

4 a place with trees and grass   _____

5 two animals   _____ _____

6 two nationalities   _____ _____

7 two types of music   _____ _____

8 two drinks   _____ _____

9 five colours   _____

D Write a description

9 Put apostrophes (') in the text.

He's short and bald, but hes got lovely blue eyes. He works in an office and he loves Italian food. He drinks red wine every weekend. He doesnt watch much TV, but he likes a good film. His names Henry – hes my dad and hes OK.

10 Think of ten adjectives in your language to describe people. Write the adjectives and the English translation. Use your dictionary.

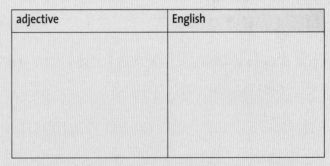

simpático, -a *adj* nice: *Es una chica muy simpática*. She's a very nice girl. ◊ *Me pareció/cayó muy ~*. I thought he was very nice.

Diccionario Oxford Pocket para estudiantes de inglés

adjective	English

11 Write a description of a friend or someone in your family. Write five sentences.

_____

_____

_____

_____

_____

12 Check your sentences for apostrophes. Do you use apostrophes in the same way in your language?

Now try the Self check on >> p.80

How to ask about prices

G countable and uncountable   **V** food and drink; prices   **P** sentence stress

A Vocabulary food and drink

1 Complete the crossword.

Across

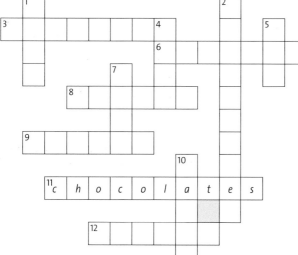

Down

B Grammar countable and uncountable

2 Write the words from the crossword in the correct box.

countable	uncountable
chocolates	

3 Add these words to the table in exercise 2.

pens perfume newspapers CDs paper
ink batteries pencils

4 Complete the questions with *is* or *are*.
1 How much _is_____ the wine?
2 How much _____ the oranges?
3 How much _____ the coffee?
4 How much _____ the newspaper?
5 How much _____ the pens?
6 How much _____ the milk?
7 How much _____ the chocolates?

5 Put the conversation in order.
A ☐1☐ How much are the biscuits, please?
A ☐ Here you are.
A ☐ OK. I'd like two cups of coffee and two packets of biscuits.
A ☐ How much is the coffee?
B ☐ Thank you.
B ☐ That's €4.60, please.
B ☐ It's €1.30.
B ☐ They're €1 a packet.

C Pronunciation sentence stress

6 6A.1▶ Listen and <u>underline</u> the stressed words.
How much are the crisps?
How much is the wine?
They're one euro twenty,
and five ninety-nine.

7 Check the audio script on » p.92. Listen again and copy the stress.

How well can you ask about prices now?
Go back to the Student's Book » p.57 and tick ✓ the line again.

How to order food in a café

g *some, any*   v food   p spellings *ee* and *ea*

A Vocabulary food

chocolatebreadchickensandwichfishsausagetomato... apple

1 Find the eight words and write them below.

1 f *ish* and chips   5 c_____ legs
2 b_____ and jam   6 a_____ pie
3 s_____ and eggs   7 t_____ salad
4 toasted s_____   8 c_____ cake

2 Write the phrases from exercise 1 in the gaps.

Dave's café	Fish	Vegetables
Meat	**Others**	
steak and chips	pizza	
	Drinks	
	tea coffee	

B Grammar *some, any*

3 Write sentences about the picture.

1 meat   *We've got some meat* .
2 eggs   *We haven't got any eggs* .
3 fish   _____ .
4 tomatoes   _____ .
5 milk   _____ .
6 cake   _____ .
7 carrots   _____ .
8 sausages   _____ .

4 Complete the conversation with these words.

any   ~~can~~   like   some   have   please   don't   would

A ¹ *Can* I help you?
B I'd ² _____ some chicken legs with tomato salad.
A Sorry, we haven't got ³ _____ chicken today – but we've got ⁴ _____ tomato salad.
B Well, can I ⁵ _____ some fish?
A With chips?
B No, thank you. I ⁶ _____ like chips.
A OK, that's fish with tomato salad. ⁷ _____ you like anything to drink?
B Just a cup of tea, ⁸ _____ .
A Thank you!

C Pronunciation spellings *ee* and *ea*

5 Say these words aloud and write them in the correct box.

~~tree~~   ~~break~~   week   speak   peas   bread   cheese
three   steak   tea   beans   please   great

/iː/	other sounds
tree	break

6 Check your answers in your dictionary. Practise saying the words.

And you? Think about your next shopping trip. What do you need?
1 *We don't need any milk.*
2
3
4
5
6

How well can you order food in a café now?
Go back to the Student's Book >> p.59 and tick ✓ the line again.

How to talk about food

G *there is, there are*   V food   P *-er* = /ə/

A Vocabulary food

1 Complete the words.

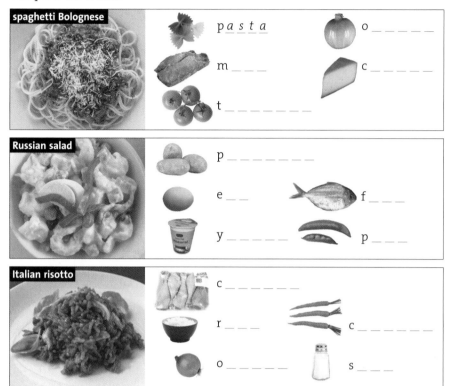

spaghetti Bolognese

p a s t a
m _ _ _
t _ _ _ _ _ _ _
o _ _ _ _ _
c _ _ _ _ _

Russian salad

p _ _ _ _ _ _ _
e _ _
y _ _ _ _ _
f _ _ _
p _ _ _

Italian risotto

c _ _ _ _ _ _
r _ _ _
o _ _ _ _ _
c _ _ _ _ _ _
s _ _ _

B Grammar *there is, there are*

A   B

2 Write sentences about the differences.

1 *In A there's some rice, but there isn't any pasta* .
2 *In B there aren't any oranges* .
3 _____ .
4 _____ .
5 _____ .
6 _____ .
7 _____ .
8 _____ .

3 Write questions with the word in brackets. Look at picture *b* and write the answers.

1 (onions) *Are there any onions?*
   Yes, there are.

2 (eggs) _____ ?
   _____ .

3 (yogurt) _____ ?
   _____ .

4 (rice) _____ ?
   _____ .

5 (apples) _____ ?
   _____ .

6 (sugar) _____ ?
   _____ .

C Pronunciation *-er* = /ə/

4 <u>Underline</u> all the words ending in *-er* and *-or*.

My sister likes an actor,

so she buys him a flower,

she sends him a letter,

but he never sends an answer.

5 **6C.1▶** Listen and repeat. Practise the /ə/ sound.

And you? What do you need to make your favourite meals? Write the ingredients. Use your dictionary if necessary.

_____
_____
_____
_____
_____
_____
_____
_____

How well can you talk about food now?
Go back to the Student's Book >> p.61 and tick ✓ the line again.

How to offer things

G *much, many, a lot of*   **V** offering phrases   **P** unstressed words *a, of, some, and, with, or*

A Grammar *much, many, a lot of*

1 Complete the sentences. Use *much, many,* or *a lot of.*

1 There _isn't much_____ butter.
2 There _____ milk.
3 There _____ eggs.
4 There _____ bread.
5 There _____ apples.
6 There _____ coffee.
7 There _____ carrots.
8 There _____ cakes.

2 Write the questions.

1 butter   _How much butter is there_____?
2 milk   _____?
3 eggs   _____?
4 bread   _____?
5 apples   _____?
6 coffee   _____?
7 carrots   _____?
8 cakes   _____?

B Vocabulary offering phrases

3 Order the words to make questions.

A coffee cup like you of would a
1 _____?

B Yes, please.

A milk take sugar you and do
2 _____?

B Just sugar, thanks.

A toast like any you would
3 _____?

B Yes, please.

A or want jam butter you do
4 _____?

B Butter is fine, thanks.

A Try these cakes – they're delicious!

B Sorry, I don't really like cakes.

C Pronunciation unstressed words *a, of, some, and, with, or*

4 Complete the phrases with these words.

like ~~butter~~ eggs water sugar pizza legs coffee

some	**bread**	and	*butter*
some	**ham**	and	_____
a	**piece**	of	_____
some	**chi**	cken	_____
some	**tea**	or	_____
with	**milk**	or	_____
What	would	you	_____ ?
a	**glass**	of	_____

... please!

5 6D.1▶ Listen and check.

6 Listen again and notice the unstressed words. Copy the pronunciation.

How well can you offer food and drink now?
Go back to the Student's Book >> p.63 and tick ✓ the line again.

A Read for detail

1 Match the words with the examples.

1. ☑ meal   a ~~breakfast, lunch, dinner~~
2. ☐ course   b apples, oranges
3. ☐ fruit   c chicken, steak
4. ☐ vegetables   d first, second, dessert
5. ☐ meat   e peas, carrots, onions

2 Read about six restaurants and answer the questions.

1. Which restaurant closes on Mondays? _4_
2. Which restaurant offers half-price food? _____
3. Which restaurants are in the same street? _____ and _____
4. Which restaurant does not offer beer or wine? _____
5. Which restaurant is not open on Sundays? _____
6. Which restaurant offers cheap drinks? _____
7. Which restaurant is expensive? _____
8. Which restaurants open every day? _____ and _____

3 Which restaurant is best for these people?

1. 'I want a cheap 3-course lunch in the city centre.' _2_
2. 'My boyfriend doesn't eat meat.' _____
3. 'I need food for six children and one adult.' _____
4. 'I want an early lunch, around eleven o'clock.' _____
5. 'My wife prefers French food.' _____
6. 'We're university students, and we'd like a cheap dinner before the film.' _____
7. 'My girlfriend loves live music.' _____
8. 'I've got only half an hour to eat before my bus leaves.' _____

4 <u>Underline</u> three or four words you don't know. Guess their meaning, and then check in your dictionary.

1

EL PASO
MEXICAN RESTAURANT

Try our famous chilli con carne!
DRINKS HALF-PRICE ON WEDS

Open 7 days a week,
12 p.m.–12 a.m.

Special prices for students

19, Kings Road (near cinema)
Tel. 347 5961

3

Portofino
Italian restaurant
Pasta, pizza, Italian wine

Special children's meals
Weds 6–7.30 all food half-price
Closed Tuesdays

44, Pebble St (next to bus station)
Tel. 837 4491

5

Oliver's café bar
47 Grant St   Tel. 394 7182

10 a.m.–2 a.m. Mon–Sat
Closed Sundays

2-course lunches €30

**Cocktails, wine, beers,
hot meals, tea, coffee**

LIVE MUSIC Tues/Wed/Thurs night
A warm welcome for everyone!

2

HOUSE OF LI
Chinese restaurant

Delicious Chinese food
3-course menu of the day €12

Open every day.
12 p.m.–2 a.m.

107 Queensway – 664 8329
(next to Central train station)

4

L'ESCARGOT
Fine French food and wine

◇◇◇◇◇◇◇◇◇◇

3-course dinner only €99

◇◇◇◇◇◇◇◇◇◇

Open Tues–Sun 6 p.m.–12 a.m.

*Please phone
to reserve your table*

14A Grant Street – 346 7195

6

Flowers
Vegetarian food

No meat, fish or eggs
No alcoholic drinks
Fresh vegetables from our own garden

**Lunches: 12–2.30
Evening meals: 6 p.m.–10.30 p.m.
Closed Wednesdays**

37 PARKSIDE – TEL. 329 4485

B Listen for general meaning

5 **6S.1►** Listen to four conversations. Number the pictures.

a
b
c
d

6 Put the first conversation in order.

A ☐ Thank you, madam.
A ☐ Would you like any wine?
A ☑ Is the food all right, madam?
A ☐ Would you like a bottle or glass?
A ☐ Red or white?

B ☐ Yes, thank you. It's fine.
B ☐ Ah, yes, please.
B ☐ Oh, er, a bottle please. A bottle of red wine.
B ☐ Red, please.

7 Check the audio script on ≫ p.92.

C Write about your favourite food

8 Complete the text with these words.
much   any   usually   ~~food~~   some

My favourite ¹_food___
is Chinese fried rice.
It's got rice, and there's
²_____ some
meat in it, ³_____
egg, different vegetables
and salt. But there isn't
⁴_____ butter in it.
The Chinese don't use butter
very ⁵_____.

9 Read about Jim's favourite food. Correct eight more spelling mistakes.

    favourite
My ~~favrite~~ food is Italian. It's called risotto and

my ant makes a delicious one. It's got rice and beens

and meet, and lots of vegetables – onyons, carots,

peaz and tomatoes. Oh, and some chease too.

And we usually have a botle of red wine with it.

10 Write five sentences about your favourite food.
*My favourite food is ...*_____
_____
_____
_____
_____

11 Check your writing for spelling mistakes.

Now try the Self check on ≫ p.81.

How to talk about free-time activities

v leisure activities

A Vocabulary leisure activities

1 Write the words.

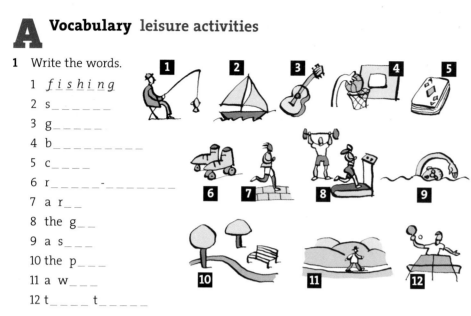

1 _f i s h i n g_
2 s _ _ _ _ _ _ _
3 g _ _ _ _ _
4 b _ _ _ _ _ _ _ _ _ _
5 c _ _ _ _
6 r _ _ _ _ _ - _ _ _ _ _ _
7 a r _ _
8 the g _ _
9 a s _ _ _
10 the p _ _ _
11 a w _ _ _
12 t _ _ _ _ t _ _ _ _ _

2 Write the words from exercise 1 in the correct box.

go	go **for**	go **to**	play	play **the**
fishing				

3 Add any more words you know.

4 Read the text and put the pictures in order.

a 1 Café
c
e
b
d
f

A relaxing weekend in the city

Well, I don't have a lot of free time. One of the first things I do at the weekend is buy a newspaper, find a café somewhere, and sit and read all the news. That relaxes me a lot. I always go for a walk, too – I need some fresh air after a week in the office, you know! And then sometimes, if I feel really active, I get my bicycle out and ride, maybe round the park, maybe in the countryside. Anything to change the routine, really. In the afternoon, I go and watch the football. After the match, I go out with my friends for a drink, usually to one of the pubs in town. And then at night we go to a disco. I love dancing. I love the music. Then on Sunday I've got another 24 hours to relax more!

5 Complete the conversation with these words.

~~often~~ go swim not
what there ever buy

A How ¹ _often_ do you have holidays?

B Usually twice a year – in August and December.

A ² _____ do you usually do?

B Well, I sometimes ³ _____ to the beach, you know.

A What do you do ⁴ _____ ?

B I often go fishing. I go for a ⁵ _____ every day, and I go to a restaurant about twice a week.

A Do you ⁶ _____ go sailing?

B No, ⁷ _____ really. It's very expensive.

A Do you ⁸ _____ gifts for your family?

B Oh, yes! Always!

And you? Answer the questions in exercise 5.
1
2
3
4
5

How well can you talk about free-time activities now?
Go back to the Student's Book >> p.67 and tick ✓ the line again.

G *Let's ..., How about ...* V weather P /w/

A Vocabulary weather

1 Look at the weather table and answer the questions.

Beijing	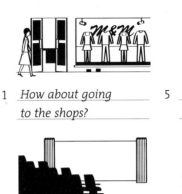	10°	**Moscow**		−10°	
Buenos Aires		26°	**New Delhi**		23°	
Cairo		44°	**Tehran**		−5°	
Jakarta		38°	**Tokyo**		13°	
Lima		24°	**Warsaw**		2°	

What's the weather like in ...

1 Tokyo? *It's rainy and cool* .
2 Cairo? _____ .
3 Lima? _____ .
4 Tehran? _____ .
5 Beijing? _____ .
6 Jakarta? _____ .
7 Warsaw? _____ .
8 Buenos Aires? _____ .
9 New Delhi? _____ .
10 Moscow? _____ .

B Grammar *Let's ..., How about ...*

2 Underline the correct words.
1 Let's <u>have</u> / having some coffee!
2 How about watch / watching TV?
3 Let's go / going for a walk!
4 How about some music / play some music?
5 Let's go fishing / fish.
6 How about go / going for a drink?
7 Let's going / go to the park!
8 How about a DVD / get a DVD?
9 Let's playing / play basketball!
10 How about reading / read in the garden?

3 Write a suggestion for each picture. Use *Let's ...* or *How about ...?*

1 *How about going*
    to the shops?

5 _____

2 _____

6 _____

3 _____

7 _____

4 _____

8 _____

4 Put the conversation in order.
A ☐ How about a game of tennis?
A ☐ Well, roller-skating is warm! Let's go roller-skating.
A 1 It's ten o'clock. What shall we do today?
A ☐ OK – **you** make a suggestion!
B ☐ I don't know. What would you like to do?
B ☐ Let's just stay in!
B ☐ Oh, it's cloudy and cold!
B ☐ I haven't got any roller-skates.

C Pronunciation /w/

5 Underline the words with the sound /w/.
<u>weather</u> what answer question windy when
snow week swim view where how why write

6 Check your answers in your dictionary. Practise saying the words.

How well can you talk about the weather and make suggestions now?
Go back to the Student's Book >> p.69 and tick ✓ the line again.

How to describe abilities

G *can, can't*; adverbs   V abilities   P unstressed *can*, stressed *can't*

A Vocabulary abilities

1 Match the verbs and the nouns.
1 play
2 ☐ climb
3 ☐ cook
4 ☐ draw
5 ☐ play
6 ☐ drive
7 ☐ speak
8 ☐ understand

a a car, a bus, a train, a lorry
b a picture, a person, an object, an animal
c another language
d eggs, fish, meat, rice, dinner
e a wall, a tree, a mountain
f a short conversation, a long text
g ~~football, tennis, basketball~~
h the piano, the guitar

B Grammar *can, can't*; adverbs

2 Complete the conversation with *can* or *can't*.

Satomi Ana! I need your help!
Ana What's wrong?
S I ¹ *can't* do my homework!
A Why not?
S I ² _____ understand this part.
A Yes, you ³ _____!
S No, I ⁴ _____! It's very difficult! ⁵ _____ you do it?
A Oh, I ⁶ _____ do it, but it's not my homework!
S Oh, please! It's late and I want to go out.
A All right, all right – let's read it together.

3 Complete the sentences with the adverbs.
1 He can speak Arabic very *slowly* . slow
2 She can climb a tree _____ . easy
3 I can skate, but not very _____ . good
4 He can drive, but _____ . bad
5 They can swim, but not very _____ . quick

4 Write sentences about Bob and Lucy.

WORK IN CHINA!
- Can you drive?
- Can you use a computer?
- Do you want to learn Chinese?

Come and work with us!

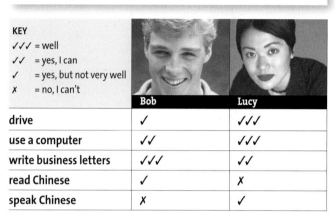

KEY ✓✓✓ = well ✓✓ = yes, I can ✓ = yes, but not very well ✗ = no, I can't	Bob	Lucy
drive	✓	✓✓✓
use a computer	✓✓	✓✓✓
write business letters	✓✓✓	✓✓
read Chinese	✓	✗
speak Chinese	✗	✓

1 *Bob can drive, but not very well* .
2 _____ .
3 _____ .
4 _____ .
5 _____ .
6 _____ .

C Pronunciation *can, can't*

5 Complete the sentences with these words.
fast   Spanish   anything   name   ~~bus~~   football

She can drive a ¹ *bus* ,
she can run ² _____ ,
and she can understand ³ _____ ,
but she **can't** cook ⁴ _____ ,
she **can't** play ⁵ _____ ,
and she **can't** remember my ⁶ _____ !

6 **7C.1▶** Listen and repeat. Copy the pronunciation of *can* and *can't*.

And you? Write five sentences about things that you can and can't do.

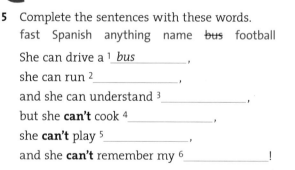

1	
2	
3	
4	
5	

How well can you describe abilities now?
Go back to the Student's Book >> p.71 and tick ✓ the line again.

How to talk about likes and dislikes

G *like doing; like sth*   V likes and dislikes   P *hate* /h/

A Vocabulary likes and dislikes

1 Fill the gaps with these verbs.

going   watching   listening to   taking   ~~meeting~~
reading   talking   playing   doing

1   *meeting*   friends, people
2   _____   homework, housework, exercise
3   _____   cards, video games, sports
4   _____   radio, music, CDs
5   _____   dancing, fishing, swimming
6   _____   to friends, on the phone, on the Internet
7   _____   TV, DVDs, football
8   _____   photos, the dog for a walk
9   _____   books, newspapers, magazines

2 Add other words you know, or look in your dictionary.

B Grammar *like doing; like sth*

3 Write the words in the correct place in the sentences.

1   I like⎮but I don't like⎮them for a walk!
    dogs, taking
    dogs, taking

2   I like on TV and I love them at the cinema.
    films, watching

3   I love to the beach but I don't like.
    going, the mountains

4   I like books but I don't enjoy.
    reading, magazines

5   I love to friends but I don't like the Internet.
    talking, using

6   I enjoy a good but I don't like!
    meal, cooking

7   I like sports but I don't like them!
    watching, playing

8   I love tea but I don't like it.
    drinking, making

9   I enjoy but I hate dog!
    eating, biscuits

4 Order the words to make questions.

A   do   cooking   like   you
    ¹ *Do you like cooking* _____?
B   Not very much!
A   cook   you   meals   what   can
    ² _____?
B   Ham and eggs, sausages, toasted sandwiches – the usual.
A   do   you   at   doing   what   like   weekends
    ³ _____?
B   Watching TV and meeting friends.
A   exercise   do   any   do   you
    ⁴ _____?
B   Not really. Sometimes I go for a swim.
A   the   you   do   holidays   enjoy   what   doing   in
    ⁵ _____?
B   Sitting on the beach with a long drink!
A   things   dislike   you   do   what
    ⁶ _____?
B   I don't like housework or homework. And I don't like listening to my daughter's music!

C Pronunciation *hate* /h/

5 **7D.1▶** Listen and underline where you hear the sound /h/.
1   Hello Henry!
2   house and home
3   half an hour
4   Who works hard?
5   She hates the housework!
6   When's your holiday?
7   I need help with my homework!

6 Listen again and repeat.

And you? Answer the questions in exercise 4.
1
2
3
4
5
6

How well can you talk about your likes and dislikes now?
Go back to the Student's Book >> p.73 and tick ✓ the line again.   43

A Listen for key information

1 7S.1▶ Listen and number the places.

- ☐ bars
- ☐ disco
- 1 hotel
- ☐ river
- ☐ car park
- ☐ gym
- ☐ park
- ☐ shops
- ☐ cinema
- ☐ hairdresser's
- ☐ restaurants
- ☐ swimming pool

2 Listen again and put the questions in order.

- ☐ All right?
- ☐ Any questions?
- ☐ OK?
- ☐ Can you see that?
- 1 Have you got that?

3 Check the audio script on ≫ p.93.

B Read and understand a brochure

4 Read the brochure and write these headings in the correct place.

Pets   Adults   Young Children   Teenagers

5 Write *true* or *false*.

1 There aren't any dance classes for young children.   *True*

2 Adults use the gym in the afternoons.   _____

3 Young children have cinema films three days a week.   _____

4 They offer study classes for adults.   _____

5 Boating is for adults.   _____

6 There are water sports for teenagers on Fridays.   _____

7 Adults have dance classes in the disco.   _____

8 Teenagers can go to the disco four nights a week.   _____

9 Young children play sports in the afternoons.   _____

10 Dogs and cats have training classes together.   _____

Holiday Out Club

1

- Water games in the children's pool, 3.00 to 6.00 every afternoon (In bad weather, these activities are in the gym)
- Sports activities in the gym, every morning from 9.00 to 10.30
- TV room with children's channels
- Reading room with comics, picture books and magazines
- Park for small children
- Lunchtime cinema, Mon Wed Fri 1.00

2

- Dance classes in the disco, mornings from 9.30 to 12.00
- Summer study classes, mornings from 9.00 to 11.00
- Water sports in the swimming pool 2.00 to 5.00 every day. Competitions at weekends (2 groups: 13–15 year-olds; 16–17 year-olds)
- Disco from 8.00 to 12.00, Thurs Fri Sat Sun
- Cinema with 5 different films every week
- Reading room with books and magazines
- Internet room

3

- Reading room with international newspapers and magazines
- Dance classes and exercises in the gym, every morning from 10.30 to 12.30 (2 groups: 18–30 year-olds; over 30s)
- Cinema with 5 different films every week
- TV and Internet room
- Boating on the river
- Fishing in the river
- Excursions

4

- Special area in the park
- Dog-walking service
- Vet available
- Training classes for you and your dog (Sat) or cat (Sun)

C Read an interview

6 Read the interview with a dancer.

Interviewer Now, Lizzie, could I just ask you ...

Lizzie Hi! My name's Lizzie Bop! I'm the star of my dance group. I want to say I just love your magazine. It's the best magazine in the shops! I really enjoy talking about myself and my life, you know?

I Thank you. Can you tell our readers about your work?

L I work very hard but I really love it. We only perform two or three nights a week, but we rehearse almost every day, sometimes for twelve hours a day. Maybe that's why I love my days off too! I like getting up late in the morning, at about eleven o'clock. I enjoy reading the newspaper and having my breakfast in bed. You see, most days I don't have time for those things.

I I see. And what else do you do when you're not working?

L I'll tell you what I don't do: I don't do the housework. I hate it! I don't really like shopping either – except for clothes, of course! – or cooking or washing the dishes. Sometimes I visit my friends and family at the weekend, but I like staying at home too. Maybe you think I'm a bit dull! I also like spending time with my dogs. I just love those dogs – they're my best friends. They can be a problem though – I have my meals in restaurants, and often they're not allowed to go in with me.

7 Tick ✓ the things Lizzie likes.
1 ☑ talking about herself   5 ☐ cooking
2 ☐ her work   6 ☐ getting up late
3 ☐ breakfast in bed   7 ☐ washing dishes
4 ☐ visiting friends   8 ☐ her dogs

8 Match the words with their meanings. Then check in your dictionary.
1 [c] star   a boring
2 ☐ perform   b told you can't do something
3 ☐ rehearse   c ~~a famous person~~
4 ☐ housework   d do something again and again to get better
5 ☐ dull   e work you do at home (cooking, cleaning ...)
6 ☐ not allowed   f do a play, concert, etc. in front of people

D Write about a day off

9 Complete the text with these phrases.
on their last day off   ~~two months~~   or play sports
half an hour   work on Sundays

João is from Portugal. Every summer he spends ¹ _two months_ picking grapes on a farm in France. The days are long, from six in the morning to six in the evening, but the workers have two hours for lunch. They also have ² _____ for breakfast at eight o'clock in the morning, and they don't ³ _____. Sunday is their day off, and they usually play music or go for a walk. They don't watch TV ⁴_____. ⁵_____, João and the others have a party and say goodbye until next year.

10 What do you do when you have a day off? Write four or five sentences.

_____
_____
_____
_____
_____

11 Check your writing for mistakes.

Now try the Self check on » p.82.

How to invite and reply

G *I'd like ..., Would you like ...?*   V social phrases   P *for* and *to*

8A

A Vocabulary social phrases

1 Complete the sentences with these phrases.

for a drink   ~~for a walk~~   to the shops
to the park   to the gym   for a coffee
to the cinema   to the pool   for a run

1 I'm going
   for a walk .

2 I'm going
   _____ .

3 She's going
   _____ .

4 She's going
   _____ .

5 I'm going
   _____ .

6 We're going
   _____ .

7 We're going
   _____ .

8 He's going
   _____ .

9 I'm going
   _____ .

2 Put the conversation in order.

A [1] Hi, Jerry. Are you busy?
A ☐ It's 11.30.
A ☐ OK, no problem.
A ☐ Yeah, I need some things.
A ☐ I'm going to the shops. Would you like to come?
B ☐ What time is it?
B ☐ Oh dear! Sorry, but I haven't got time. I need to start cooking lunch!
B ☐ No, not really. Why?
B ☐ The shops?

B Grammar *I'd like ..., Would you like ...?*

3 Underline the correct words.
1 Would you like dance / to dance?
2 I'd like a drink / drinking.
3 They'd like to go to Paris / go for Paris for the weekend.
4 Would you like a coffee? / have coffee?
5 Would you like go out / to go out for a meal?
6 We'd like an apple / having an apple.
7 She'd like be / to be alone.
8 I'd like go a walk / a walk.
9 Would you like going / to go to the park?

C Pronunciation *for* and *to*

4 Complete the sentences with *for, to, four,* or *two*.
1 A We usually have a snack at about *four* o'clock.
  B It's ten _____ four now. Let's eat!

2 A We're going _____ the football match.
  B Oh! I'd love _____ go _____ the match!

3 A We're going _____ a sandwich. Would you like one?
  B I'd like _____ please! One ham, one cheese.

4 A We're going _____ a drink! Would you like _____ come?
  B I'd love _____ come, but I've got _____ exams tomorrow – English and maths.

5 **8A.1▶** Listen and read the audio script on ≫ p.93.

6 Listen again and notice the different pronunciation of *for / four* and *to / two*.

46

How well can you invite and reply now?
Go back to the Student's Book ≫ p.77 and tick ✓ the line again.

How to **say what to wear**

G imperatives V family; clothes P *shirt* /ɜː/ or *short* /ɔː/

A Vocabulary family; clothes

1 Complete the sentences.

Lucy   Bernard   Michael   John   Helen   Theresa

Lucy and John are sister and brother.

1 *Michael* _____ is Bernard's father.
2 _____ is Helen's uncle.
3 _____ is Bernard's aunt.
4 _____ is John's brother-in-law.
5 _____ is Theresa's nephew.
6 _____ is Michael's niece.

2 Write the words.

1 j*eans*_____ and a T-_____
2 a sh_____ and t_____
3 a h_____ and c_____
4 a j_____ and tr_____
5 sh_____ and s_____
6 b_____ and sh_____
7 a s_____ and a dr_____
8 a sh_____ sk_____ and
   a l_____ sk_____
9 a sw_____ and a c_____

B Grammar imperatives

3 Match the instructions with the signs.
Use your dictionary.

1 [c] Cross the street!
2 ☐ Don't cross the street!
3 ☐ Don't swim here!
4 ☐ Drive this way!
5 ☐ Don't drive this way!
6 ☐ Leave your pets outside!
7 ☐ Don't use your mobile phone!
8 ☐ Don't smoke in here!
9 ☐ Don't make fires here!
10 ☐ Be careful!

C Pronunciation *shirt* /ɜː/ or *short* /ɔː/

4 8B.1▶ Listen and underline the correct words.
1 I can't find my shirts / shorts!
2 We're going to work / walk this afternoon.
3 What's that bird / board on the tree?
4 She lives on the third / fourth floor.
5 Mum! Where are my football shorts / shirts?
6 What time do you start working / walking?
7 Smith! Is this your board / bird?
8 What's the third / fourth country on the map?

5 Listen again and repeat.

> **And you?** Answer the questions.
>
> 1 What are you wearing today?
> _____
> 2 What are your favourite clothes for winter?
> _____
> 3 And for summer?
> _____

How well can you say what to wear now?
Go back to the Student's Book >> p.79 and tick ✓ the line again.   47

How to say what's happening

G present continuous +|-|? V action verbs P *-ing* /ɪŋ/

A Vocabulary action verbs

1 Write the *-ing* form of the verbs.

1 sit   *sitting*   4 look at _____   7 smile _____

2 drink _____   5 play _____   8 use _____

3 laugh _____   6 dance _____   9 write _____

B Grammar present continuous +|-|?

2 Complete the sentences with the present continuous. Use the verbs in exercise 1.

1 He *'s sitting* on a desk.

2 She ____ _____ to the music.

3 He ____ _____ .

4 ____ she _____ in a notebook?

5 ____ he _____ the phone?

6 She ____ _____ computer games.

7 He ____ _____ .

8 They ____ _____ photos.

9 He ____ _____ coffee.

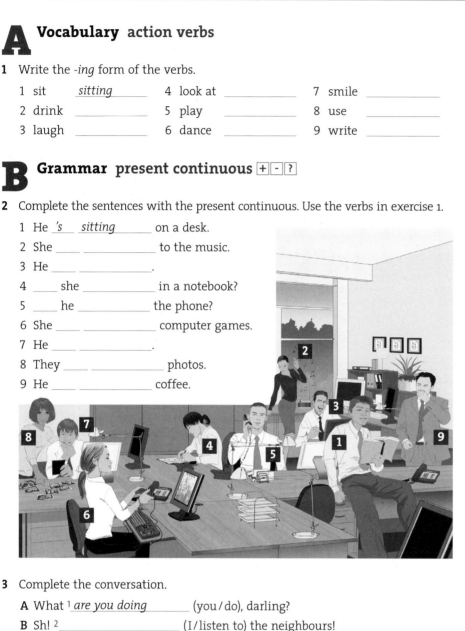

3 Complete the conversation.

A What ¹*are you doing* (you/do), darling?

B Sh! ² _____ (I/listen to) the neighbours!

A What ³ _____ (they/do)?

B Mrs Jones ⁴ _____ (talk) to someone.

A What ⁵ _____ (she/say)?

B ⁶ _____ (she/talk) to Mr Jones.

   Oh, ⁷ _____ (they/talk) about us!

C Pronunciation *-ing* /ɪŋ/

4 Complete the phrases with these words.

bath bike car exercises dinner ~~nothing~~ park speaking you

1 something – anything – *nothing*

2 reading – writing – _____

3 driving a _____

4 walking in the _____

5 riding a _____

6 making _____

7 doing _____

8 having a _____

9 thinking about _____

5 **8C.1▶** Listen and check. Repeat all the phrases.

And you? Answer the questions. Use your dictionary if necessary.

1 When do you go dancing?

   I often go dancing at the weekend.

2 Do you usually write letters or emails? _____

   _____

3 What do you drink when you go out? _____

   _____

4 What sports do you play?

   _____

   _____

5 Where in the classroom do you usually sit? _____

   _____

6 What makes you laugh?

   _____

   _____

How well can you say what's happening now?
Go back to the Student's Book >> p.81 and tick ✓ the line again.

How to describe actions

G present simple and present continuous P contrastive stress

A Grammar present simple and present continuous

1 Underline the correct words.

1 Usually, Tench gets up / is getting up at 8.00,
   but today she's having / she has breakfast at 8.00.
2 Today is different. Today she doesn't go / isn't going
   to work.
3 She always is taking / takes a notebook,
   but today she's taking / she takes a map, too.
4 She usually arrives / is arriving at work at 9.00,
   but today she's going / she goes to the airport.
5 It's 11.00 and she waits / is waiting for someone.
   Usually she is having / has a coffee break at 11.00.
6 Most days she looks / is looking at a computer screen.
   Today she looks at / is looking at a man's face.
7 She normally is going / goes home after work,
   but today she flies / is flying to another country.
8 She is having / has an interesting day today!

2 Complete the text with the verbs in brackets in the present simple or present continuous.

Onderkofer is a special agent. His life is interesting – he ¹ _meets_ (meet) a lot of people, he ² _____ (travel) to different places, and he ³ _____ (eat) different food. The only problem is that his work is a secret. He can never tell people what he is really doing when he meets them.

Anyway, today he's in Prague, in the Czech Republic. Today he's a tourist: he ⁴ _____ (wear) jeans and boots, a pink shirt and glasses. He ⁵ _____ (carry) a camera and a guide book. He's got a meeting at eleven o'clock. At 10.45, he is in a café near the church. There are three people inside. One man is at the window. He ⁶ _____ (drink) coffee. A woman near the door ⁷ _____ (write) in a notebook. Another man ⁸ _____ (watch) the TV on the wall. He ⁹ _____ (wear) jeans and boots, a pink shirt and glasses, and has a camera and guide book too. Onderkofer looks and looks at the man. 'What ¹⁰ _____ (you do) here?' he asks him.

B Pronunciation contrastive stress

3 Complete the sentences with these words.

he she ~~they~~ him her us
~~us~~ her him they she he

1 **We**'re watching **them**, but _they_ aren't watching _us_ .
2 **He**'s looking at **her**, but _____ isn't looking at _____.
3 **She** likes **him**, but _____ doesn't like _____.
4 **He** always phones **her**, but _____ never phones _____!
5 **We** sometimes invite **them**, but _____ don't invite _____!
6 **She** talks about **him**, but _____ doesn't talk about _____.

4 8D.1▶ Listen and check. Copy the stress.

And you? Complete the sentences.
1 Usually I wear _____, but today I'm wearing _____ _____.
2 Usually I do my homework _____, but today I'm doing it _____.
3 Usually I _____, but today _____.

Unit 8 Skills Practice

A Read for detail

1 Read the text. Are the tips for men (M), women (W) or men and women (MW)?

Dress for *Success*

Is it important how you dress at an interview? Is it OK to wear jeans and a T-shirt? Jenny Tinker is an interviewer for a big London company. She thinks it is very important! 'Some people come to an interview in the wrong clothes,' she says. 'I never give a job to a man in shorts and sandals, a woman in a miniskirt, or anyone in jeans.' Here are ten tips to help you in your next interview.

1 Wear a suit and tie for an interview for an office job.
  M

2 Wear dark shoes and clean them before the interview.
  MW

3 Take off your hat before you sit down.
  _____

4 Wear a jacket and a long skirt or trousers.
  _____

5 Don't wear a lot of jewellery.
  _____

6 Don't wear jeans. You are going to an interview, not to the pub!
  _____

7 Don't wear a very short skirt.
  _____

8 Have a normal hairstyle, and it's good if it's not green!
  _____

9 Don't wear a lot of aftershave.
  _____

10 For an interview for a factory job, wear comfortable, clean clothes – but not jeans!
  _____

2 Write *true* or *false*.

1 It's good to wear black jeans, but not blue ones. *False*
2 Jenny Tinker thinks how you dress at interviews is important. _____
3 It is OK to clean your shoes in the interview. _____
4 A long skirt is good, but not a short skirt. _____
5 Green hair is good for interviews. _____
6 Leave your hat at home. _____
7 Yellow shoes are good, but not black ones. _____

3 Underline three or four words you don't know. Guess their meaning, and then check in your dictionary.

B Listen for detail

4 **8S.1▶** A spy is watching a man in the station. Listen and tick ✓ the man he is describing.

5 Listen again. Complete these phrases with the adjectives you hear.

1 a *tall* _____ man
2 _____ _____ hair
3 a _____ _____ coat
4 a _____ tie
5 _____ shoes

6 Check the audio script on ≫ p.93.

C Read film reviews

7 Match the texts and the pictures.

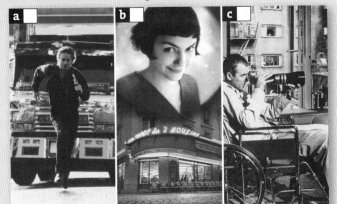

1 Rear Window
Alfred Hitchcock, 1954

Starring James Stewart   **RATING** *****

THE STORY: A man lives in his apartment in a wheelchair. He can't walk, run or stand. He spends all his time sitting in his wheelchair, looking out of the window. He can see many of the neighbours in their apartments. He can see them cooking, eating, playing with their children – and arguing. One day, he sees a man argue with his wife, and then he can't see the wife. He thinks the man kills his wife ...

THE ACTORS: In my opinion, Stewart is excellent ...

2 Black Rain
Ridley Scott, 1989

Starring Michael Douglas   **RATING** ***

THE STORY: An American policeman travels to Japan with a Japanese criminal. But the criminal escapes in the airport, and the policeman helps the Japanese police to find him again ...

THE ACTORS: Douglas is another American policeman with a big motorbike ...

3 Amélie
Jean-Pierre Jeunet, 2001

Starring Audrey Tautou   **RATING** ****

THE STORY: Amélie lives alone and works in a café. She sees the same customers every day and she often thinks about a different life – a life with love. She spends a lot of time making other people happy. But then she meets a man ...

THE ACTORS: Audrey Tautou is superb as Amélie ...

8 Match the words with the meanings. Then check in your dictionary.

1 [c] wheelchair
2 ☐ argue
3 ☐ criminal
4 ☐ escape
5 ☐ superb

a talk in an angry way with someone
b get away from somebody, e.g. a policeman
c ~~a chair with wheels for someone who can't walk~~
d very good
e a person who does something against the law

D Write a review

9 Complete the text with these words.

love   got   has   puts   boring   ~~is~~

Film title: **Diva**

Year: 1981
Director: Jean-Jacques Beineix

■ **THE STORY:** Jules ¹ *is* a postman. He is in ² _____ with Cynthia, who is an opera singer (she is the Diva). He ³ _____ a lot of problems when somebody ⁴ _____ a video tape in his postbag.

■ **THE FILM:** This is a marvellous film. It's ⁵ _____ love and action. The film is fresh, and never ⁶ _____. I really love the photography.

10 Read the text. <u>Underline</u> three more adjectives.

Film title: **Snakes On A Plane**

Year: 2006
Director: David R. Ellis

■ **THE STORY:** Hundreds of <u>dangerous</u> snakes are on a plane, and so is an FBI agent, Neville Flynn (Samuel L. Jackson). He is taking an important witness to Los Angeles. Only Flynn can save the plane and kill the snakes before they kill all the terrified passengers.

■ **THE FILM:** This is a silly film – you can enjoy the action and have a good laugh.

11 Think of a film you know well. Write a short review.

Film title: _____

Year: _____   Director: _____

Write three sentences about the story:

_____

_____

_____

_____

Write three sentences about why you liked or didn't like the film:

_____

_____

_____

_____

12 Check your sentences for mistakes. Can you add one or two adjectives?

Now try the Self check on >> p.83.

How to ask for transport information

v transport; instruction phrases   **P** polite intonation

A Vocabulary instruction phrases

1 Match the places and the instructions. Start at the Gare du Nord.

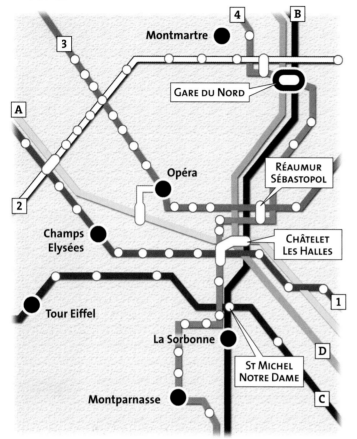

1   *c*   Take the B or D train line south to Châtelet Les Halles. Change to the metro, Line 1. Get off at the fifth stop west.

2   ☐   Take the metro, Line 4, south. It's 13 stops after that. You don't need to change trains.

3   ☐   Take the B train line south. It's one stop after St Michel Notre Dame.

4   ☐   Take the B train line south to St Michel Notre Dame. Change to another train, the C line, and travel west. It's the fourth stop.

5   ☐   Take the metro, Line 4, north. Get off at the next stop. Change to Line 2, and go west. Get off at the next stop, and walk from there.

6   ☐   Take the metro, Line 4, south. Get off at Réaumur Sébastopol. Change to Line 3, and go west. It's the fourth stop.

   a   Opéra   d   Tour Eiffel
   b   Montmartre   e   Montparnasse
   c   ~~Champs Elysées~~   f   La Sorbonne

B Vocabulary transport

2 Write the transport words.

1   *departure gate*

6

2

7

3

8

4

9

5

C Pronunciation polite intonation

3 **9A.1▶** Listen. Do the speakers sound polite (P) or rude (R)?
1   ☒ R   Excuse me, how can I get to the museum, please?
2   ☒ P   Excuse me, how can I get to the museum, please?
3   ☐   Excuse me, how can I get to the airport, please?
4   ☐   Excuse me, how can I get to the airport, please?
5   ☐   Excuse me, how can I get to the hospital, please?
6   ☐   Excuse me, how can I get to the hospital, please?
7   ☐   Excuse me, how can I get to the park, please?
8   ☐   Excuse me, how can I get to the park, please?

4 Listen again. Copy the polite intonation.

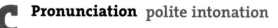

How well can you ask for transport information now?
Go back to the Student's Book >> p.87 and tick ✓ the line again.

How to give and follow directions

v places in town; directions **P** linking words together

A Vocabulary places in town

1 Complete the crossword.

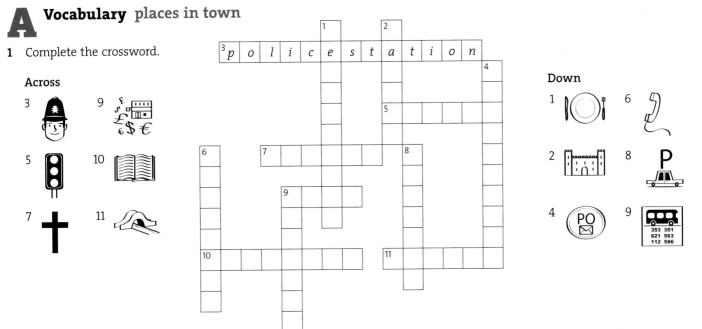

Across

3

9

5

10

7

11

Down

1

6

2

8

4

9

B Vocabulary directions

2 Complete the directions.

1 from the bank in Argyle Street to the health centre:
Go along Argyle Street _to_ Mitchell Street.
Turn _left_ , and go _____ on. It's at the _____
corner _____ the left.

2 from Glasgow Bridge to St Enoch shopping centre:
Go along Jamaica Street and turn _____ into
Howard Street. Go straight _____ and it's on
the _____ .

3 from St Enoch underground station to the post office:
Go _____ of the station into Argyle Street, and
_____ left. The post office is _____ the
corner _____ the bank.

C Pronunciation linking words together

3 **9B.1▶** Listen. Where one word ends with a consonant sound and the next word begins with a vowel sound, write ‿.

1 It's the first left‿at the corner.

2 There's a bank at the corner.

3 The post office is just opposite.

4 Go straight on and turn left at the lights.

5 The map says there's an art gallery near here.

6 It's across the bridge and on the left.

7 Turn right again into Union Street.

8 I think there's a tourist information office in the station.

4 Listen again and repeat. Do you link words like this in your language?

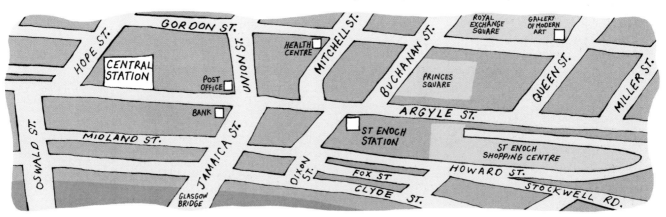

How well can you give and follow directions now?
Go back to the Student's Book >> p.89 and tick ✓ the line again.

How to ask about and describe a holiday

G past simple of be +-? *was, were, wasn't, weren't* V adjectives; holidays P *is, was, are, were*

A Vocabulary adjectives; holidays

1 Cross out the wrong adjective.

1 The weather is lovely warm ~~noisy~~ horrible
2 The people are boring unfriendly crowded polite
3 The beach is crowded quiet polite empty
4 The hotel is clean comfortable wet expensive
5 The room is small dirty uncomfortable friendly
6 The food is uncomfortable cheap delicious awful
7 The shops are expensive full delicious boring
8 The nightlife is empty fantastic cheap awful

2 Write these adjectives in the correct box.

~~clean~~ ~~dirty~~ lovely beautiful comfortable horrible boring unfriendly polite exciting uncomfortable awful delicious interesting fantastic

positive	negative
clean	dirty

B Grammar past simple of be +-? *was, were, wasn't, weren't*

3 Complete the conversation with *was, were, wasn't,* or *weren't.*

A ¹ *Were* you in another country?
B Yes, I ² _____.
A ³ _____ you alone?
B No, I ⁴ _____.
A ⁵ _____ your boyfriend with you?
B Yes, he ⁶ _____.
A ⁷ _____ you on a beach?
B No, we ⁸ _____.
A ⁹ _____ you in the mountains?
B Yes, we ¹⁰ _____.
A What ¹¹ _____ the weather like?
B It ¹² _____ very cold!
A ¹³ _____ you walking in the mountains?
B No, we ¹⁴ _____.
A ¹⁵ _____ you skiing?
B Yes, that's right! We ¹⁶ _____ skiing!

C Pronunciation *is, was, are, were*

4 Complete the phrases with *is* or *are.*

The beach __*is*__ nice
The boys _____ fun
The water _____ warm
In the holiday sun
But my parents _____ here
But my parents _____ here

5 Complete the phrases with *was* or *were.*

The food __*was*__ good
The weather _____ great
The drinks _____ cheap
The bars opened late
But our daughter _____ there
But our daughter _____ there

6 9C.1▶ Listen and check.

7 Listen again and repeat. Notice the pronounciation of *is, was, are,* and *were.*

And you? Answer the questions about your last holiday.

1 Where were you? _____
2 Were you in a hotel? _____
3 Was there any rain? _____
4 Were the people nice? _____
5 What was the food like? _____
6 Would you like to go back? _____
7 Why / why not? _____

How well can you ask about and describe a holiday now?
Go back to the Student's Book >> p.91 and tick ✓ the line again.

How to **tell a story**

G past simple ⊞ regular *-ed*   P *-ed* endings

A Grammar past simple ⊞ regular *-ed*

1 Write the past forms of these verbs.

1 happen *happened*
2 look _____
3 notice _____
4 relax _____
5 walk _____

6 decide _____
7 stay _____
8 play _____
9 talk _____
10 want _____

2 Complete the story with the verbs from exercise 1.

Holidays? Don't talk to me about holidays! We had a terrible holiday last year. Let me tell you what ¹*happened*. We ²_____ a different holiday, so we ³_____ to go camping. We ⁴_____ at a campsite near the beach. It was a beautiful place, very quiet. We ⁵_____ a lot. We went fishing and swimming, and we went sailing on some small boats. It was great!

One day after lunch, the children ⁶_____ in the water, and we ⁷_____ together outside the tent. Later we ⁸_____ to the village. We ⁹_____ at the shops, we had coffee and then it was time to go back to the tent. But the tent wasn't there! Then we ¹⁰_____ two things: nobody else had their tents near the water, and there was something red in the sea. Our tent? Oh no! That was our tent in the sea!!

3 Order the words to make the beginning of *Nightmare Hotel*.

1 up I walked hill the
   I walked up the hill
2 Hotel to Nightmare the
   _____
3 at I door the stopped
   _____
4 I see couldn't but bell the
   _____
5 knocked waited I and I
   _____
6 the windy cold in and night
   _____
7 in window looked the I
   _____
8 there but any wasn't light
   _____

B Pronunciation *-ed* endings

4 Complete the sentences with these words.

town   ~~bus stop~~   umbrella
way   rain   help   question

He waited at the
 *bus stop*_____.

It started to
_____.

He opened his
_____.

A voice asked him to
_____.

He answered her
_____.

They walked into
_____.

They talked all the
_____.

And who knows what happened after that!

5 **9D.1▶** Listen and check. Repeat the *-ed* verbs.

A Read about a holiday

1 Match the pictures and the words. Use your dictionary.

1 a bear 2 a coast 3 a cork 4 an island 5 a skull

2 Read the text and draw the route on the map.

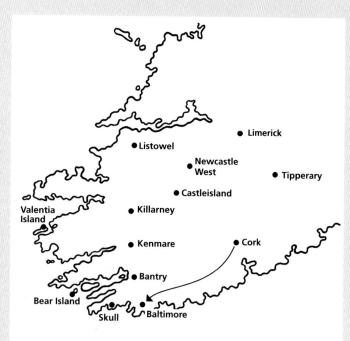

My friends went to Ireland last summer to visit the
beautiful west coast. They started their holiday at Cork.
They stayed there for two days and visited the church
and the shops. They also went by bus to Blarney Castle.
Then they travelled by car to Baltimore and spent a
day fishing. The next day they went to the town of
Skull. There they travelled by boat and sailed round
to Bear Island. The weather was good there, so they
went for a long walk. Their next stop was Valentia
Island on the famous Ring of Kerry. They wanted
to watch animals in the sea, but it rained all day.
It rains very often in this part of Ireland! After that,
they stopped at Castleisland, where they had lunch.
Then they went to Newcastle West to visit some friends,
and finally they arrived at Limerick. There they played
golf, and visited the castle and the gift shops. They
enjoyed their holiday very much!

3 Match 1–8 with a–h?

1 ☑ *d* Baltimore   a They went for a walk.
2 ☐ Bear Island   b They visited friends.
3 ☐ Castleisland   c They played golf.
4 ☐ Cork   d ~~They spent a day fishing~~.
5 ☐ Limerick   e It rained a lot.
6 ☐ Newcastle West   f They went sailing.
7 ☐ Skull   g They went to the church.
8 ☐ Valentia Island   h They had lunch.

B Listen for general meaning

4 9S.1▶ Listen to Sarah talking about her holiday in France.
Put the events in order.

a ☐ travelled into the mountains
b ☐ arrived at the youth hostel
c ☐ watched a woman working
d ☐ talked a lot
e ☑ *1* travelled to Lyon

5 Write *true* or *false*.

1 Sarah's flight was expensive.   *False*
2 She got a flight to Lyon.   _____
3 She travelled east into the mountains.   _____
4 She met a friend from work.   _____
5 Her friend's name was Brian.   _____
6 It rained every day.   _____

6 Listen again and complete the text.

Well, I went to France *last* _____, on a _____
_____. I stayed in youth hostels, you know, where
_____ _____ _____ lots of _____ _____,
and they tell you all the _____ to visit.

7 Check the audio script on ⟩⟩ p.93.

C Read and understand a story

8 Read the story and put the paragraphs in order.

a ☐ On her first day, she and the other tourists left the hotel early in the morning on a special safari bus. They went with a guide, and he answered all their questions. Everyone had their cameras ready to take photos of the animals.

b ☐1 My friend Dana's a dentist. She works hard and makes a lot of money. She isn't married and she hasn't got any brothers or sisters, so she's got a lot of free time. Maybe that's why her favourite hobby is travelling.

c ☐ Everyone was worried because the elephants were very big, and the bus was very small. But then something incredible happened. One of the elephants pushed the bus out of the mud and onto the road. The tourists smiled and laughed, and Dana took some wonderful photos.

d ☐ Dana visits a different country every year, and last year she decided to go to Africa, to Kenya. She wanted to go on safari, to see the wild animals there.

e ☐ Suddenly there was a problem. The bus was stuck in the mud. It couldn't move forwards or backwards. And then three enormous elephants appeared. The tourists were very happy and took lots of photos. But then the elephants came near the bus and the tourists were all quiet.

9 Match the words with their meanings.

1 [e] guide   a   something you like doing when you aren't working
2 ☐ hobby
3 ☐ worried   b   can't move
4 ☐ stuck   c   very big
5 ☐ mud   d   soft wet earth
6 ☐ enormous   e   ~~person who shows and tells you about a place~~
   f   unhappy about something that could happen

D Write about holidays

10 The highlighted words are spelled wrong. Can you correct them?

                            uncle

When I was 14, my family, my aunt and oncle, and my my cosins all visited Portugal. It was our first holiday in another contry, and it was very exciting. We stayed in a big house with a swimming pool. The people were very frenly, the weather was sunny and hot, and the food was delicous. We went for long walks on the beech, my mother and my ant did some shopping, and my father read his books. We all bought gifts to take home. It was an espensive holiday, but not for me – I didn't pay for it!

11 Are the highlighted words nouns or adjectives? Use your dictionary.

   Example

> **uncle** ○━ /ˈʌŋkl/ *noun*
> the brother of your mother or father, or the husband of your aunt: *Uncle Paul*

Oxford Essential Dictionary

12 Think about a holiday when you were a child. Make notes in the table.

How old were you?	
Where did you go?	
Who did you go with?	
What were the people like?	
What was the food like?	
What was the weather like?	
What did you do?	
What did you like?	

13 Write about your holiday.
   When I was ... _____

_____

_____

_____

14 Check your writing for spelling mistakes.

Now try the Self check on >> p.84.

How to continue a conversation

G past simple ? wh- questions   P stress in wh- questions

 A Grammar past simple ?

1 Match the questions and answers.
1 *f* When was the last time you went away?
2 ☐ Where did you go?
3 ☐ Where did you stay?
4 ☐ Who did you meet?
5 ☐ Did they have a good time?
6 ☐ Did you see anything interesting?
7 ☐ Did you buy anything?
8 ☐ When did you come home?

a They said the weather wasn't very good.
b Yes, we bought some gifts in the village.
c We met some friends there.
d Yes, we saw a lot of animals.
e We came back late on Sunday evening.
f ~~A month ago, in May.~~
g We stayed in a hotel.
h We went to the mountains.

2 Write questions for the missing information.

The schoolchildren went away for the day last week. They went to ¹_____. They spent all day in the town. First they visited the ²_____ and they enjoyed it a lot. Then they met ³_____, a famous TV personality. Fantastic! They asked her ⁴_____ and she told them some very interesting stories. At one o'clock they had lunch, but the children said ⁵_____. In the afternoon, they went shopping. Julia bought ⁶_____ for her parents and spent a lot of money. Finally, they went to the cinema and saw a new film. Julia said it was a bit boring! They arrived home ⁷_____, and went straight to bed.

1 Where   *did the schoolchildren go*   ?
2 What   _____   ?
3 Who   _____   ?
4 What   _____   ?
5 What   _____   ?
6 What   _____   ?
7 When   _____   ?

3 Match the answers with the questions in exercise 2.
a *1* To Dublin.
b ☐ Gifts.
c ☐ It wasn't very good.
d ☐ Tina Green.
e ☐ The museum.
f ☐ A lot of questions.
g ☐ After ten o'clock.

B Pronunciation stress in wh- questions

4 Match the sentences with the responses.
1 *b* I met my new boss this morning!
2 ☐ They went to a Thai restaurant.
3 ☐ My brother phoned.
4 ☐ We went shopping yesterday.
5 ☐ His children were on TV!
6 ☐ My parents are here.
7 ☐ She went away last summer.
8 ☐ It's not raining now.

●	●	●	●
a **When**	did	they	**come?**
b **What**	did	you	**think?**
c **What**	did	they	**eat?**
d **Where**	did	she	**go?**
e **What**	did	you	**buy?**
f **What**	did	they	**do?**
g **When**	did	it	**stop?**
h **What**	did	he	**say?**

5 **10A.1▶** Listen and check. Copy the stress.

And you? Answer the questions in exercise 1.

1	
2	
3	
4	
5	
6	
7	
8	

How well can you continue a conversation now?
Go back to the Student's Book >> p.97 and tick ✓ the line again.

How to talk about a career

G past simple regular and irregular   **V** careers   **P** *wrote* /t/ or *rode* /d/

A Grammar past simple regular and irregular

1 Write the past simple form of the verbs.

1 leave *left*
2 buy _____
3 drive _____
4 get _____
5 have _____
6 join _____
7 become _____
8 meet _____
9 see _____
10 sell _____
11 start _____
12 work _____

2 Complete the text with the past simple verbs from exercise 1.

Chuck ¹*left* school when he was 16. He ²_____ a job as a bus driver, but then he ³_____ an accident. Later, he ⁴_____ as a waiter for three years. He ⁵_____ a girl in the restaurant, and they got married. Unfortunately, they got divorced ten months after that, when he ⁶_____ his wife in a car with another man. Chuck ⁷_____ the army to forget his problems, but he ⁸_____ an army lorry into a river, and went back to normal life. A few months later, he got money from an aunt, ⁹_____ a restaurant and ¹⁰_____ his own business. Five years after that, he ¹¹_____ rich and ¹²_____ the business. Now he's writing a book about his life.

B Pronunciation *wrote* /t/ or *rode* /d/

3 **10B.1▶** Listen and underline the correct word.
1 He wrote / rode home.
2 She rides / writes like an adult.
3 We send / sent her a gift for her birthday.
4 That's Batman / a bad man!
5 It's a hard / heart job!
6 They went to town / down this morning.

4 Check the audio script on ≫ p.94. Listen again and repeat.

C Vocabulary careers

5 Complete the phrases.

1 a l e f t school
  b got a j__ as a l_____ dr_____
  c dr___ a l_____ for five years
  d b_____ his own l____

2 a w___ to u_____
  b became a t_____
  c w____ abroad
  d got m_____

How to talk about what happened

G past simple ⊟⊡ **P** *didn't*

A Grammar past simple ⊟⊡

1 Complete the sentences with these verbs in the past simple, first in the positive and then in the negative.

write ~~ride~~ pay get drink leave put

1 He _rode_ his bike to school, but he _didn't ride_ it home.

2 He _____ an MP3 player for his birthday, but he _____ a computer.

3 She _____ the workers, but she _____ them well.

4 They _____ tea and coffee, but they _____ any alcohol.

5 She _____ to her father, but she _____ to her brother.

6 He _____ poison in the food, but he _____ it in the drinks.

7 We _____ the room, but we _____ the hotel.

2 Read the conversation. Order the words to make questions.

Ana I saw a really good TV programme last night.

Satomi it about was what

¹_What was it about_ ?

A It was about a woman who was angry with her husband.

S angry she was why

2 _____ ?

A He always came home late. She didn't know where he was.

S do did what she

3 _____ ?

A She called a private detective.

S her he tell did what

4 _____ ?

A He told her the man was with another woman.

S did the what do wife

5 _____ ?

A She killed her husband!

S poison did use she

6 _____ ?

A No. She prepared a bath for him.

S bath die in husband her the did

7 _____ ?

A Yes! His wife pushed an electric fan into the water.

S body do she did what the with

8 _____ ?

A Nothing – she called the police.

S police the say she did what to

9 _____ ?

A She said it was an accident.

S end the happened what in

10 _____ ?

A I don't know! The next part is on tonight.

S Ooh! What channel?

3 Complete the policeman's questions.

1 Where / go yesterday _Where did you go yesterday_ ?
I went to work.

2 When / finish work _____ ?
I finished at six o'clock.

3 go straight home _____ ?
No, I didn't. I went shopping first.

4 Which shops / visit _____ ?
A lot of shops. I don't remember the names.

5 Who / meet _____ ?
Nobody.

6 kill your husband _____ ?
No, of course not!

B Pronunciation *didn't*

4 **10C.1▶** Listen and repeat the poem. Notice that *didn't* is stressed.

Tommy was a **wai**ter
Who **didn't** like his **boss**
He **didn't** really **hate** her
But he **didn't** keep his **job**

How well can you talk about what happened now?
Go back to the Student's Book >> p.101 and tick ✓ the line again.

How to talk about life stories

v years; education   **P** /s/ or /z/

 A **Vocabulary** education

1 Complete the crossword.

Across

4   e = mc²

6

13

7   When you are eleven or twelve, you go to s_____ school.

9   You get this qualification after you study for three or four years at university.

14   When you are four or five you go to p_____ school.

Down

1

2   Good morning / Bonjour / Buenos días

3   In some places, secondary school is called h_____ s_____.

8

5   For example, Oxford, Harvard, La Sorbonne.

10   You can get this qualification if you study for one or two years

12

11   1789 / 1917 / 1939–45

2 Complete the sentences with words from the crossword.

1   She studied l *iterature* for two years and got a di_____.

2   He did four years of c_____ at u_____ and got a d_____.

3   She studied h_____ at h_____ s_____ but she didn't like it very much.

B **Vocabulary** years

3 Write the years in words.

Year	You say ...
1969	*nineteen sixty-nine*
2006	
1908	
1836	
1998	
1950	
2025	

C **Pronunciation** /s/ or /z/

4 **10D.1▶** Listen and underline the words you hear.

/s/	or	/z/
1 <u>Greenpeace</u>	or	green peas
2 blue ice	or	blue eyes
3 Police!	or	Please!
4 Yes, Miss	or	Yes, Ms
5 a place in the theatre	or	plays in the theatre
6 this book	or	these books

5 Check the audio script on ≫ p.94. Listen again and repeat.

And you? Answer the questions.

1   Where did you go to school / college / university?
_____

2   What did you study? _____

3   What were your favourite subjects?
_____

4   What subjects didn't you like?
_____

How well can you understand and talk about life stories now?
Go back to the Student's Book ≫ p.103 and tick ✓ the line again.

Unit 10 Skills Practice

A Read and understand a life story

1 Read about Edvard Munch and complete the text with these phrases.

for the next 20 years
when he was 17
at age 18
when he died in 1944
~~when he was a boy~~

Edvard Munch was born in a small town in Norway in 1863. ¹_When he was a boy_, his family moved to the capital, Oslo. His mother died when he was five, and then he also lost one of his brothers and a sister. ²_____, he went to university to study engineering, but he had health problems. Then the next year, ³_____, he decided to change career and become a painter. He studied art for about four years before moving to Paris in 1885.

⁴_____, he lived between Paris and Berlin. This is when he painted *The Scream*, his most famous picture. When he was 45, he had more health problems, and went back to live in Norway. His life changed, and his paintings became less pessimistic. ⁵_____, the city of Oslo built a museum for his art. In 2004, thieves stole *The Scream* from the museum, but police found the painting in 2006.

2 Guess the meaning of the highlighted words. Check in your dictionary.

3 Read the text again. Write *true* or *false*.
1 Munch was born in Oslo. _False_
2 His mother, brother and sister died. _____
3 He studied art after he went to Paris. _____
4 He returned to Norway when he was ill. _____
5 He built a museum for his paintings. _____

B Listen for detail

4 **10S.1▶** Listen and answer the questions.

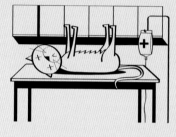

1 What <u>didn't</u> she try to kill the vet with?

  a ☐ a gun   b ☐ poison   c ☐ a knife

2 How many times did she try?
  a ☐ two
  b ☐ three
  c ☐ four

3 What happened in the end?
  a ☐ she escaped
  b ☐ the vet died
  c ☐ the police got her

5 Listen and put the questions in order.
  a ☐ Why not?
  b ☐ So what did she do?
  c ☐1☐ And?
  d ☐ She shot him?
  e ☐ So did she kill him in the end?
  f ☐ Didn't she stop then?

6 Read the summary. Listen again and correct four more mistakes.

     cat
The ~~dog~~ was sick, so the woman took it to the doctor's clinic, but it died. She tried to kill the vet, first with poisoned apples, second with a poisoned magazine, and third with a knife.

7 Check the audio script on ≫ p.94.

C Read a job advert

8 Write the headings in the correct place.
 a You get   b Applications to   c You need

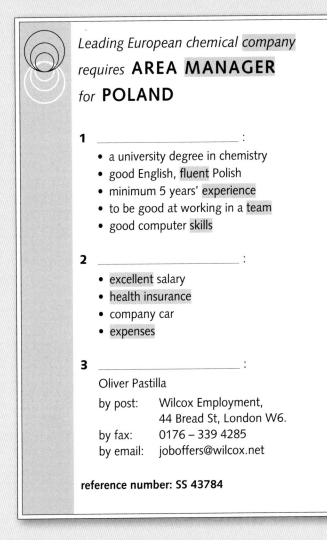

Leading European chemical company

requires **AREA MANAGER**

for **POLAND**

1 _____ :
- a university degree in chemistry
- good English, fluent Polish
- minimum 5 years' experience
- to be good at working in a team
- good computer skills

2 _____ :
- excellent salary
- health insurance
- company car
- expenses

3 _____ :

Oliver Pastilla

by post: Wilcox Employment,
            44 Bread St, London W6.
by fax: 0176 – 339 4285
by email: joboffers@wilcox.net

reference number: SS 43784

9 Match the highlighted words in the advert with the definitions.

1 everything you learn from doing a job _experience_
2 a business organization _____
3 speaks a language very well _____
4 money for hotels and restaurants _____
5 you don't pay for doctors or hospitals _____
6 very good _____
7 a group of people who work together _____
8 abilities/things that you can do well _____
9 a person who organizes the work of other people
_____

10 Check your answers in your dictionary.

D Write biodata

11 Read about Sonia Gandhi and complete the text with *and* or *but*.

SONIA GANDHI was born in the north of Italy in 1946. In 1964, she met Rajiv Gandhi in Cambridge. Sonia [1] _and_ Rajiv were both students. The couple got married four years later, [2] ____ moved to India. Sonia [3] ____ Rajiv had two children, a boy [4] ____ a girl. Sonia became an Indian citizen in 1983. Many people in the Gandhi family were politicians, [5] ____ Rajiv was different. He worked as a pilot and Sonia worked at home. In 1982, Rajiv started a career in politics. Two years later someone assassinated his mother, the Indian prime minister. The Gandhi family had a history of tragedy, [6] ____ Sonia's husband was also assassinated in 1991. In 1998, Sonia finally began a career in politics and today she is the leader of a large political party.

12 Match the words with their meanings. Then check in your dictionary.

1 [c] citizen   a a person who flies a plane
2 [ ] pilot   b a person at the top of a group
3 [ ] assassinate   c ~~a person with the nationality of a country~~
4 [ ] tragedy   d kill an important or famous person
5 [ ] leader   e a very sad event

13 Think of a person who is important for you. Make notes in the table below.

Topic	your person
born	
early life	
education	
work	
now	

14 Now write five or six sentences of biodata. Remember to use *and* or *but*.

_____
_____
_____
_____

15 Check your writing carefully.

Now try the Self check on >> p.85.

How to make suggestions

G *too big, not big enough*   V holiday accommodation; suggestions   P stress in long words

A Vocabulary holiday accommodation

1 Find six types of holiday accommodation and write them below.

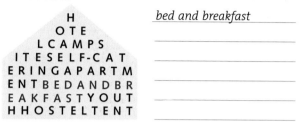

H
O T E
L C A M P S
I T E S E L F - C A T
E R I N G A P A R T M
E N T B E D A N D B R
E A K F A S T Y O U T
H H O S T E L T E N T

bed and breakfast
_____
_____
_____
_____
_____

2 Complete the sentences with the holiday accommodation in exercise 1.

1 Let's stay in a *bed and breakfast*. We can eat lunch and dinner in town.

2 I love sleeping in a _____ when we go camping.

3 We can't stay in a _____ – I'm too old.

4 The _____ has everything we need, and there's space for 200 tents.

5 I don't like staying in a _____, because I don't want to cook and clean on holiday.

6 Let's stay in a 5-star _____. We can stay in bed all day and get room service!

B Grammar *too + adjective; not + adjective + enough*

3 Complete the sentences with *too* or *not enough* and the adjective.

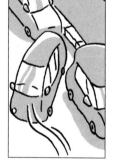

1 This room *isn't warm enough*. warm

2 The ring *is too expensive*. expensive

3 The parking space _____. big

4 My tea _____. hot

5 This place _____. dirty

6 This taxi _____. slow

7 This museum _____. interesting

8 This place _____. quiet

9 The shops _____. far

C Pronunciation stress in long words

4 **11A.1▶** Listen and write the number of syllables.

1 adjective   _3_   5 interview   ____
2 conversation ____   6 sentences   ____
3 exercise   ____   7 syllables   ____
4 information ____   8 vocabulary   ____

5 Write the words in the correct box.

●●●	●●●●	●●●●●
adjective		

6 Listen again and repeat.

How well can you make suggestions now?
Go back to the Student's Book >> p.107 and tick ✓ the line again.

How to say what's wrong

G *too much / many, not enough*   **V** rooms and furniture   **P** long and short vowel sounds

A Vocabulary rooms and furniture

1 Complete the estate agent's advert with these words.

bath   chairs   cooker   cupboard
fridge   shower   sink   sofa   table
~~toilet~~   washbasin

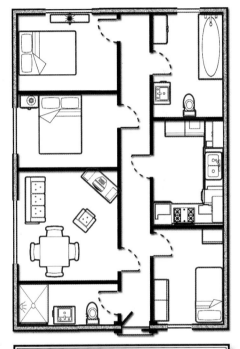

FASBUCKS
· ESTATE AGENT ·

TO RENT
large flat near town centre

3 bedrooms (2 double, 1 single)

First bathroom with [1]t*oilet*____,
[2]b_____, washbasin,
and [3]c_____

Second bathroom with toilet,
[4]sh_____ and [5]w_____

Living room with [6]s_____,
[7]t_____, [8]ch_____
and TV

Kitchen with [9]s_____,
cupboards, [10]fr_____,
and [11]c_____

B Grammar *too much / many* + noun, *not enough* + noun

2 Ana and Satomi are having a party for 20 people. Write sentences with *too* and *enough*.

1 *There aren't enough*____ tables.
2 *There are too many*____ chairs.
3 _____ juice.
4 _____ wine.
5 _____ food.
6 _____ glasses.
7 _____ CDs.
8 _____ space for dancing.

C Pronunciation long and short vowel sounds

3 Write these words in the correct box. Use your dictionary.

~~gym~~   ~~stay~~   ~~view~~   town   golf   beach   park   tea
shop   walk   sink   hot   farm   drive   pub

short vowel sound	long vowel sound	
1 vowel symbol	2 vowel symbols	1 vowel + :
gym /dʒɪm/	*stay* /steɪ/	*view* /vjuː/

4 Practise saying the words.

And you? Write an estate agent's advert for your home.

_____
_____
_____
_____

How to **compare things**

G comparatives **V** adjectives **P** *-er* endings

A Vocabulary adjectives

1 Find ten adjectives in the puzzle and match them with the opposites.

H	E	L	G	E	L	S	M	A	L	L
C	C	N	D	S	E	T	A	X	E	W
C	O	M	F	O	R	T	A	B	L	E
L	L	O	A	F	W	M	N	L	Z	X
F	D	D	D	T	S	S	L	L	R	P
Q	D	E	O	V	O	O	O	O	O	E
A	P	R	N	M	T	H	I	N	S	N
M	O	N	E	W	L	T	G	G	E	S
D	O	A	B	R	H	R	S	H	E	I
X	D	I	R	T	Y	X	T	E	D	V
I	S	E	A	P	T	I	G	N	E	E

1 hard   *soft*
2 warm   _____
3 short   _____
4 old-fashioned _____
5 big   _____
6 clean   _____
7 old   _____
8 fat   _____
9 cheap   _____
10 uncomfortable _____

B Grammar comparatives

2 Underline the correct words.
1 His brother's fater/<u>fatter</u> than he is.
2 Cities on the north coast are cooler/more cool than cities in the south.
3 My bed is more comfortable/comfortabler than the hotel bed.
4 Your room is more warm/warmer than my room.
5 Tom is better/more good than Harry.
6 That table is dirtyer/dirtier than our table.
7 John's dog is more small/smaller than the neighbour's dog.
8 The new bridge is longer/more long than the old one.

3 Compare Frank's car and Ricky's car. Use these adjectives.
~~fast~~ dirty comfortable old good expensive bad

Frank

Ricky

1 *Ricky's car is faster than Frank's* _____ .
2 _____ .
3 _____ .
4 _____ .
5 _____ .
6 _____ .
7 _____ .

C Pronunciation *-er* endings

4 **11C.1▶** Read and listen to the poem.
<u>Underline</u> the words that end in *-er*.

Winter sleep
The days become shorter not longer
The weather becomes colder not warmer
Inside is warmer than outside
His eyes become smaller then close
Sleep the winter sleep
Wait for a better life in the spring

5 Listen again and repeat the poem.

And you? Write two things you have which are:	
1 warm	*my coat, my jacket*
2 new	
3 expensive	
4 old-fashioned	
5 dirty	
6 soft	
7 cheap	
8 comfortable	
9 modern	

How well can you compare things now?
Go back to the Student's Book >> p.111 and tick ✓ the line again.

How to understand opinions

G superlatives **V** furniture; adjectives **P** /w/ /v/ /b/ /p/

A Vocabulary furniture; adjectives

1 Match the furniture and the rooms. Some words match more than one room.

sofa chair dining table desk coffee table
~~bed~~ table shelf

1 bedroom _bed_

2 living room _____

3 kitchen _____

4 office _____

2 Write more furniture words in each place. Use your dictionary.

3 ~~Cross out~~ the wrong adjective.

1 This is a very comfortable / expensive / ~~fast~~ sofa.

2 His car is the most modern / happiest / most old-fashioned in our street.

3 Your brother is the biggest / oldest / lowest student in the class!

4 Brian's desk is the strongest / fastest / most modern in the office.

5 Which is the most exciting / most relaxing / most useful bar in town?

6 That's the best / strongest / worst newspaper I know.

7 Which train is the most modern / fastest / softest?

8 In summer, Biarritz is the most useful / most expensive / most attractive place on the coast.

9 In many countries, the bus is the cheapest / most useful / strongest kind of transport.

B Grammar superlatives

4 Write the superlative form of the adjectives.

1 cheap _the cheapest_

2 long _____

3 short _____

4 modern _____

5 old-fashioned _____

6 hot _____

7 cool _____

8 high _____

9 low _____

10 expensive _____

5 Write superlative sentences. Use the adjectives from exercise 4.

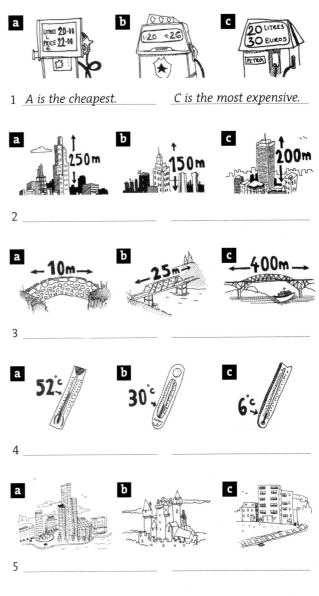

1 _A is the cheapest._   _C is the most expensive._

2 _____

3 _____

4 _____

5 _____

C Pronunciation /w/ /v/ /b/ /p/

6 Complete the phrases with w, v, b, or p.

1 a _b_ottle of _w_ine

2 a _late of _eans

3 a _iece of _a_er

4 a _onderful _iew

5 a _hite _athroom _ash_asin

6 we ha_e _ink, white, or _lack shel_es

7 Check the audio script on ≫ p.94.

8 **11D.1▶** Listen and repeat.

Unit 11 Skills Practice

A Read and understand travel tips

1 Read about travelling in India. Match the headings with the paragraphs.

People Clothes Accommodation Transport Food

2 Match the highlighted words with the definitions.

1 not cheap but not too expensive   _____
2 the money you can spend on your holiday   *budget*_____
3 a plant we use to make clothes   _____
4 to keep you safe   _____
5 a kind of meat   _____
6 before the date you want to travel   _____

3 Check the information. Write *true* or *false*.

1 It's difficult to buy food when you travel by train.   *False*_____
2 In India you need to drive on the left.   _____
3 There are no youth hostels in India.   _____
4 It's a good idea to wear nylon clothes.   _____
5 There's excellent vegetarian food in India.   _____
6 People in the north often eat with their hands.   _____
7 It's safe to drink all kinds of water.   _____
8 English is the main language in India.   _____

Visit... India

1 _____

The question is: do you have a big budget or a small budget?
By air: flights are available between the major cities in India.
By train: trains are the most popular transport for long distances. They're cheap but always very busy. Buy your ticket four or five days in advance. Don't worry about food – people sell food at all the stations.
By bus: cheap but always crowded.
By bicycle: cheap and healthy, but don't forget that in India people drive on the left!

2 _____

You can find everything from five-star hotels in the big cities and tourist attractions to small family-run hotels at reasonable prices. Youth hostels are also cheap, clean, and friendly. In smaller towns, it's a good idea to see the room before you decide.

3 _____

Cotton is good for the high temperatures, but nylon can be very uncomfortable. If you're visiting the mountains in the north, take warm clothes. Remember: the higher you travel, the cooler the temperature at night. For your feet, take sandals for the hotter areas and the coast, and boots for the mountains. A hat or cap to protect your head is also a good idea.

4 _____

Indian cooking is one of the wonders of the world! In the south, there are delicious vegetarian dishes with rice or potatoes. Remember that people in the south often eat with their hands. You find meat dishes more often in the north. Don't forget the lamb dishes and cold yogurt drinks. One other important thing: it is safest to drink bottled water.

5 _____

Everyone outside of the big cities is friendly if you try to communicate with them. Language can be a problem – there are 17 main languages – but you can usually find someone who speaks English.

B Read a catalogue

4 Write these words in your language. Use your dictionary.

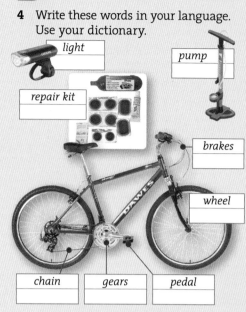

light
pump
repair kit
brakes
wheel
chain
gears
pedal

5 Look at the information and answer the questions.

a RACING BIKE — €250
▶ weight 14 kg
▶ 16 gears
▶ Pump, repair kit, and lights not included

b TOURING BIKE — €200
▶ weight 20 kg
▶ 12 gears
▶ Pump and lights included

c MOUNTAIN BIKE — €350
▶ weight 16 kg
▶ 24 gears
▶ aluminium frame
▶ Pump, repair kit, and lights not included

1 Which bike has space for bags?   *b*
2 Which is the most expensive?   _____
3 Which is the lightest?   _____
4 Which one has the most gears?   _____
5 Which one includes a pump in the price?   _____
6 Which one do you prefer?   _____

C Listen for detail

6 Match the words and pictures. Use your dictionary if necessary.

1 ☐ fridge	4 ☐ microwave	6 ☐ kitchen			
2 ☐ heating	5 ☐ toilet paper	7 ☐ towels			
3 ☐ pillows					

7 **11S.1▶** Listen to a man talking about a problem. Tick ✓ the words you hear in exercise 6.

8 Listen again and choose the best answer.

1 The angry man is in:
  a his car   b a hotel   c an apartment

2 The man says he has _____ problems.
  a four   b five   c six

3 The reason for the problem is:
  a the man   b the telephone   c the receptionist

9 Match the objects and the problems.

1 ☐ fridge	a there aren't enough
2 ☐ kitchen	b there isn't any
3 ☐ toilet paper	c it doesn't work
4 ☐ heating	d it's dirty
5 ☐ towels	e it's too hot

10 Listen again and complete the sentences.

1 My family and I are in apartment number six, and
  we _____ _____ _____ _____ .

2 Just a moment please. Could you _____ _____
  _____ slowly?

3 Now, could you just give _____ _____ _____ ?

4 And what time _____ _____ _____ at the apartment?

5 And what's the _____ _____ _____ apartment?

11 Check the audio script on ≫ p.94.

D Write about your home

12 Complete the text with these phrases.

a lot of noise   from the living room
from the shops   ~~a quiet part of town~~

We live in a flat in ¹ *a quiet part of town* . It's
five minutes walk from the park and ten minutes
² _____. There isn't much traffic,
and there aren't too many neighbours, so there isn't
³ _____. We live on the fourth floor,
and we can see the river ⁴ _____.

at the other end   the biggest room
one of the walls   opposite the TV

My favourite room is the living room. It's
⁵ _____ in the flat and it's where we
spend most of our time. There's a comfortable sofa on
one side, ⁶ _____ and the bookshelves.
At one end there's a dining table and chairs, and
⁷ _____ a glass door that opens on to
the balcony. There's a coffee table in the middle, and
there are lots of photographs on ⁸ _____.
I love looking at the photographs and remembering the
people and places.

13 Write about your home. First, describe the location of your home, and second, your favourite room.

I live ... _____

_____

_____

_____

_____

My favourite room is ... _____

_____

_____

_____

_____

_____

14 Check your writing for mistakes. Show your writing to another student and read his or hers. How can you make yours better?

Now try the Self check on ≫ p.86.

A Vocabulary signs

1 Complete the crossword.

Across   Down

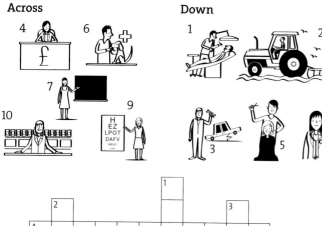

4 6
7
10 9
3 5 8

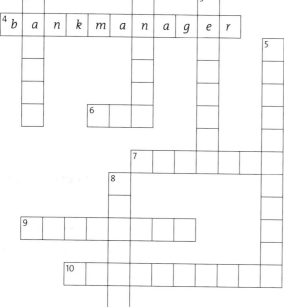

⁴ b a n k m a n a g e r

2 Complete the sentences with words from exercise 1.

1 If I don't know the price, I ask the *shopkeeper*.
2 If I need an eye test, I go to the _____.
3 When I need some extra money, I talk to the
   _____.
4 If I get toothache, I go to see the _____.
5 When my dog isn't well, I take him to see the
   _____.
6 When my hair's too long, I visit the _____.
7 If the car doesn't work, I make an appointment
   with the _____.
8 If my son has a problem at school, I talk to his
   _____.

B Vocabulary times of the day

3 Look at Emma's diary. Answer the questions with these expressions.

tomorrow night   mid-morning tomorrow
first thing tomorrow morning   early tomorrow evening
late tomorrow morning   ~~mid-afternoon tomorrow~~
the day after tomorrow

MON	TUES	WED
TODAY	8.30 cleaning lady	
	10.30 doctor	
	11.30 bank	11.30 shopping
	15.00 mechanic	
	19.00 hairdresser	
	21.30 theatre	

1 When does Emma's car go to the mechanic?
   Mid-afternoon tomorrow   .
2 When does the cleaning lady arrive?
   _____.
3 When is her appointment with the doctor?
   _____.
4 When is her appointment with the bank manager?
   _____.
5 When does she go shopping? _____.
6 When is her appointment with the hairdresser?
   _____.
7 When does she go to the theatre? _____.

C Pronunciation intonation to ask and confirm

4 **12A.1▶** Listen and write A (ask) or C (confirm).
1 [C] The dentist's   6 [ ] Nine-thirty
2 [A] The dentist's   7 [ ] An hour later
3 [ ] On Friday morning   8 [ ] An hour later
4 [ ] On Friday morning   9 [ ] For coffee
5 [ ] Nine-thirty   10 [ ] For coffee

5 Check the audio script on ≫ p.94.

6 Listen again and copy the pronunciation.

How well can you make an appointment now?
Go back to the Student's Book ≫ p.117 and tick ✓ the line again.

How to say how you feel

v the body; health **P** short and long vowels

A Vocabulary the body

1 Complete the instructions.

1 Put your two h*ands* on your h*ead*.
2 Put your right h_____ on your st_____, and your left h_____ on your b_____.
3 Put your h_____ between your l_____, and your h_____ on your f_____.
4 Put your right f_____ on your h_____, and your left a_____ round your n_____.
5 Put your two h_____ on your b_____.
6 Put your two f_____ round your n_____, and your h_____ on your st_____.
– and count to 100!

B Vocabulary phrases to say how you feel

2 Match the problems.

1 [c][ ][ ] I feel   a it's a headache
2 [ ]   I don't feel   b back pains
3 [ ][ ] I think   c ~~terrible~~
4 [ ][ ] I've got   d well
                          e really ill
                          f a stomach ache
                          g awful
                          h it's flu

3 Match the suggestions.

1 [b][ ][ ] Don't   a a day off
2 [ ][ ]   Stay   b ~~get up~~
3 [ ][ ]   Take   c some medicine
                     d go out
                     e at home
                     f in bed
                     g go to work

4 Complete the conversation with these words.

headache don't fine housework much ache
with ~~wrong~~

A Hello! What's ¹ *wrong*_____ with you?
B I've got a stomach ²_____. I think I ate too ³_____ last night.
A Hmm. Why ⁴_____ you take some medicine?
B I don't like medicine!
A Yes, but this is very good! Take it ⁵_____ a glass of water. ... Is that better?
B Hey, yes! I feel ⁶_____ now!
A That's great! You can get up and do the ⁷_____.
B Oh no! I think I'm getting a ⁸_____.

C Pronunciation short and long vowels

5 Say these words aloud and write them in the correct box.

~~hat~~ ~~heart~~ cat hand arm back car start
half park

Short vowel sound /æ/	Long vowel sound /ɑː/
hat	heart

~~leg~~ ~~stay~~ friend pain head twelve they
game weather eight

Short vowel sound /e/	Long vowel sound /eɪ/
leg	stay

6 Check your answers in your dictionary. Practise saying the words.

How well can you say how you feel now?
Go back to the Student's Book >> p.119 and tick ✓ the line again.

71

How to talk about future arrangements

G present continuous future **P** sentence stress in questions

A Grammar present continuous future

1 Write the verbs in the continuous form.

1	do	_doing_	6	play	_____
2	prepare	_____	7	put	_____
3	go	_____	8	come	_____
4	have	_____	9	take	_____
5	cook	_____	10	help	_____

2 Complete the conversations with the correct form of *be* + a verb from exercise 1.

Satomi So what ¹_are_ you _doing_ this weekend, Jim?

Jim Oh, lots of things! My weekend starts early – ²I'____ _____ at a children's party this afternoon.

S Oh yeah?

J Yeah, it's my niece's birthday, and I promised I would go. But ³I'____ _____ dinner for friends this evening, so I have to go to the shops later. What about you?

S Me? Oh, ⁴I'____ _____ away for the weekend. We want to visit Wales. ⁵We'____ _____ the six o'clock train to Cardiff.

J Really? I hope you have a good time!

Mark Are you busy tomorrow, Ana?

Ana Er, yeah. ⁶I'____ _____ tennis mid-morning, and then in the afternoon my friend ⁷____ _____ to stay for a few days. What are you doing?

M ⁸We'____ _____ a party on Saturday night, and wanted to know if you'd like to come.

A Great! I'd love to! Do you need any help?

M Well, ⁹we'____ _____ most of the furniture in another room so there's enough space to dance. ¹⁰We'____ _____ everything mid-afternoon, so if you can come about that time, that would be great. You can bring your friend too!

A OK. Why don't you give me the address?

3 Ivan and Marina are on holiday in Bali. Complete the sentences.

Activities programme

Monday
Go shopping in Ubud, the artists' village
Drive to Lake Batur

Tuesday
Have lunch at Singaraja
Visit the water temple at Bedugul

Wednesday
Buy gifts at the market in Denpasar
Have dinner at Kuta Beach
Watch dance performance at Sanur

Bali

1 On Monday, they _are going shopping_ in Ubud.
2 After that, they _____ to Lake Batur.
3 On Tuesday, they _____ at Singaraja.
4 After lunch, they _____ the temple at Bedugul.
5 On Wednesday, they _____ in Denpasar.
6 In the evening, they _____ at Kuta Beach.
7 At night, they _____ a dance at Sanur.

B Pronunciation sentence stress in questions

4 12C.1▶ Listen and copy the stress.

1 **What** are you **do**ing next **week**?
  Where are you **go**ing?
  Who are you **meet**ing?
  What are you **eat**ing?

2 **When** are you **go**ing on **hol**iday?
  Where are you **stay**ing?
  What are you **do**ing?
  Who are you **tak**ing?

And you? Answer the questions in exercise 4.

1 _____
_____
_____
_____
2 _____
_____
_____
_____

How well can you talk about future arrangements now?
Go back to the Student's Book >> p.121 and tick ✓ the line again.

How to talk about intentions

G *going to* for future intentions   V lifestyle   P fast speech

A Grammar *going to* for future intentions

1 Complete the questions and answers using *going to*.

1 What *are you going to be* (be) when you grow up?

I _____ (not / be) a doctor.

I _____ (be) a footballer!

2 Where _____ (go) on holiday?

We _____ (visit) the north of Germany.

We _____ (not / stay) in the south.

3 What _____ (do) with the car?

He _____ (drive), so

he _____ (not / drink).

4 What _____ (study) at university?

I _____ (think) about it for a while.

I _____ (not / decide) until next year.

2 Read Cathy's notes. Write *I* for intention, or *A* for arrangement.

1 Phone Helen
   I

2 meet John at the airport, Fri 9 p.m.
   A

3 go shopping with Mum Thursday morning
   ____

4 take children to dentist for their appointments
   ____

5 have parents' meeting at school Fri 4.30
   ____

6 work in the garden
   ____

7 go to Paula's wedding
   – Sat 11.30 a.m.
   ____

8 Sit down and relax!
   ____

3 Write complete sentences for the notes. Use *going to* or present continuous.

1 *She's going to phone Helen* .

2 *She's meeting John at the airport on Friday* .

3 _____ .

4 _____ .

5 _____ .

6 _____ .

7 _____ .

8 _____ .

B Vocabulary lifestyle

4 Match 1–8 with a–h.

1 ☐d quit   a weight
2 ☐ get   b chess
3 ☐ do   c a gym
4 ☐ lose   d ~~smoking~~
5 ☐ join   e fit
6 ☐ play   f some exercise
7 ☐ eat   g green tea
8 ☐ drink   h healthy food

C Pronunciation understand fast speech

5 **12D.1▶** Listen and write *F* (fast) or *N* (normal).

1 ☐N She doesn't want to go.
2 ☐F She doesn't want to go.
3 ☐ He's going to stop smoking.
4 ☐ He's going to stop smoking.
5 ☐ I want to leave early today.
6 ☐ I want to leave early today.
7 ☐ They aren't going to listen to you!
8 ☐ They aren't going to listen to you!

6 Check the audio script on ≫ p.94. Practise saying the fast sentences.

And you? What are you going to do to be healthier and happier?	
1 stop doing?	*I'm going to stop …*
2 start doing?	_____
3 eat?	_____
4 drink?	_____
5 learn?	_____
6 play?	_____

Unit 12 Skills Practice

A Listen for detail

1 **12S.1▶** Listen to four people making appointments. Complete the table.

	Place	Day	Time
1	bank		
2			
3			
4			

2 Match the questions with the conversations.

a ☐ When would you like the appointment?
b ☐ That's Friday, isn't it?
c ☑ Did you say Tuesday?
d ☐ What's the problem?
e ☐ Eleven o'clock?
f ☐ Is that the bank?
g ☐ Did you say seven o'clock?
h ☐ Twelve o'clock on Monday?

3 Listen to the first conversation again. Put the words in order.

1 I'd like to make an _____ .
manager speak the to please to appointment

2 One moment please. OK, _____ ?
which were day thinking you of

3 Some time _____ .
week this the weekend before

4 Right, thank you Mr Brunel. That's next _____

_____ .
eleven Thursday in at morning the

4 Check the audio script on ≫ p.94.

B Read for detail

5 Read the notes and complete Mark's diary.

Hi, Helen!

Sorry, Monday night I'm studying – I've got an exam first thing the next morning. Are you going to Satomi's party on Tuesday night? Maybe see you there.

Mark

****

Hi Mark,

We're going out for a drink on Monday night. Do you want to come with us?

Helen

Baybridge Dental Clinic

34 Kenwood Drive, Chester
Tel. 0725 339-4168

Your next appointment:

Tuesday 27th April, 12.00 p.m.

Mark!
Don't forget – it's your turn to clean the kitchen and bathroom on Wed morning!

John

Mark
You weren't here when I called. Are you still OK for lunch on Wed at Blake's – and the cinema at 8.30?
Call me! Paula

Mark,
Remember you're going to help me choose your father's present on Monday! See you at the Main St. exit in the shopping centre at 1.30.
Love, Mum

Chester Amateur Football Club

NEXT MATCH:
Tues 27th, 4 p.m.

(Meet at the park 3.30)

---

26 Monday	27 Tuesday	28 Wednesday
9–12 classes	Morning _____	Morning _____
1.30 _____	12.00 _____	1.00 _____
night _____	3.30 _____	8.30 _____
	4.00 _____	
	night _____	

C Read adverts

6 Write these words in the adverts.

garage   hairdresser's   optician's   supermarket

a

Gateways

The country's favourite

Special offers every day!
Look for the prices in red.

**FRESH FOOD AT
FABULOUS PRICES.**

Order by phone or on the Internet
Open Mon–Sat 9 a.m.–9 p.m.
Sundays 11 a.m.–5 p.m.
Car park 200 spaces
Tel. 685-2219

www.gateways.net

b

Waves 'n' Curls

Welcome to your local

_____

– for men and women.

**This week's special offer:
one FREE child's haircut
for every adult customer.**

By appointment only

Open
Mon–Sat 9 a.m.–6 p.m.
Tel 685-4395

(Closed Wednesdays)

c

Insight

_____

If you can't read these
adverts, we can help!!

*All kinds of glasses
and contact lenses.
The best selection in town.
Reading glasses from only £10.
Come and see us!*

Open Mon–Fri 9.30–5.30

45 South St.
(opposite the post office)

d

MORRISONS

_____

✓ **We repair all kinds of car.**
✓ **Fast and reliable service.**

FREE OIL CHANGE
WHEN YOU MAKE
AN APPOINTMENT.

Call for an appointment now:
Tel. 685-7791

67 Bute St. (next to cinema)

7 Answer the questions.

1 Which place closes on Wednesdays?   *b*
2 Which two places have special offers?   _____ and _____
3 What time does the optician's close?   _____
4 Which place has its own website?   _____
5 What do I get if I make an
   appointment at the garage?   _____
6 Where can I order by phone?   _____
7 How much do reading glasses cost?   _____
8 Which place is nearest to the cinema?   _____

8 Underline three words you don't know. Guess their
meanings, and check in your dictionary.

D Write a letter

9 Read the wedding invitation. Complete Maika's reply
with these words.

company   happy   ~~invitation~~   love   say
show   wonderful

Linda Spencer and David Taylor
would like you to
come to their wedding
on Saturday 28 July 2007
at two o'clock
at St. Mary's Church
Lemon Tree Walk
Oxford
and afterwards at the Welcome Hotel, Oxford

Dear Linda,

Thank you very much for the ¹ *invitation* to your
wedding. I was very ² _____ to hear your
news. I would ³ _____ to go to the wedding,
but my ⁴ _____ is sending me to
South America for a week, and I really can't
⁵ _____ no! Maybe you can ⁶_____
me the wedding photographs when I come back.
I hope you have a ⁷ _____ day!
Best wishes,
Maika

10 Imagine you get this invitation to a party, but you can't
go. Write your own letter.

Please come to Satomi's birthday party.

Place: 25 Barnton Road
Date: Friday 27th September
Time: 10 p.m.
       Bring a bottle!

Dear Satomi,
_____
_____
_____
_____
_____

11 Check your writing for mistakes.

Now try the Self check on >> p.87.

Unit 1 Self check

Grammar

1 Complete the text with these words.

I'm   name's   is   my   my   number's   is

My ¹_____ John Evans. ²_____ from York in England. England ³_____ in Britain, in Europe. I'm British. I speak English. ⁴_____ address ⁵_____ 18 Park Street. ⁶_____ phone ⁷_____ 837 7382.

2 Underline the correct word.
1 What is / are your name?
2 Where are you / your from?
3 What's / What your address?
4 How / What old are you?
5 What is you / your email address?

Vocabulary

3 Write the numbers.

1	11	*eleven*	5	19 _____
2	3	_____	6	55 _____
3	17	_____	7	76 _____
4	8	_____	8	12 _____

4 Order the words to make sentences and questions.
1 name   your   what's   me   excuse

_____?

2 jim@teleline.uk   address   his   is   email

_____.

3 for   thanks   coffee   the

_____.

4 it   spell   you   how   do

_____?

5 phone   my   is   91 456 2110   number

_____.

Pronunciation

5 Write the letters with the same sound in the correct box.

~~j~~   v   i   l   k   b   n   f   d

a	m	t	y
j	_____	_____	_____
_____	_____	_____	_____

Check your answers on ›› p.88.

What are you going to do now?
a Nothing. I'm happy.
b Revise grammar / vocabulary / pronunciation and try again.
c Ask another student / my teacher for help.

To revise go to …
Student's Book Review ›› p.15   Grammar Bank ›› p.136
Workbook ›› pp.4–7   www.oup.com/elt/result

Reading

Read these texts again.
> Workbook ›› p.8 exercise 1
> Workbook ›› p.9 exercise 9

How confident are you?
I can understand …
- [ ] some words
- [ ] with help
- [ ] when I read again
- [ ] everything

Listening

Listen to this audio again.
> Workbook ›› p.8 audio script 1S.1▶

How confident are you?
I can understand …
- [ ] some words
- [ ] with help
- [ ] when I listen again
- [ ] everything

Writing

Do this writing exercise again.
> Workbook ›› p.9 exercise 11

How confident are you?
I can write …
- [ ] with help
- [ ] on my own
- [ ] with some mistakes
- [ ] with no mistakes

What are you going to do now?
a Nothing. I'm happy.
b Ask my teacher for help.
c Practise my reading / listening / writing.

To practise go to …
Student's Book ›› pp.6–14
Workbook ›› pp.8–9
MultiRom Listening section
www.oup.com/elt/result

Unit 2 Self check

Grammar

1 Add 's to complete the text.

Hi! My name Max. I'm from Canada. I'm eighteen years old and I live with my parents. My mother name Sara and she a doctor. My father name Jed and he a driver.

2 Complete the sentences with these possessives.

our my their his her your

1 Kemal's parents live in Turkey. _____ house is in Izmir.
2 John's brother is a singer. _____ name is Steve.
3 We live in London. _____ address is 12 Eaton Street.
4 Thomas, what is _____ mother's name?
5 Rita is from Spain but _____ husband is English.
6 I'm from Ireland. _____ name's Michael.

Vocabulary

3 Complete the sentences with these words.

married rich old single young divorced

1 Their daughter is very _____. She's three.
2 My brother is _____. His wife's name is Eleanor.
3 David is _____. He has a big apartment in New York.
4 He's an _____ man. He's seventy-five.
5 He is not her husband now. They are _____.
6 My sister's 25 and she's not married, she's _____.

4 Complete the phrases with the correct word.

1 10.30   h_____ past ten
2 11.15   q_____ past eleven
3 5.50   t_____ to six
4 6.40   t_____ to seven
5 12.00 a.m.   m_____

Pronunciation

5 Say the words aloud. <u>Underline</u> the stressed syllable.

Example <u>twen</u>ty

1 thirty   5 nineteen
2 fifty   6 seventeen
3 sixteen   7 forty
4 ninety   8 fourteen

Check your answers on >> p.88.

What are you going to do now?

a Nothing. I'm happy.
b Revise grammar / vocabulary / pronunciation and try again.
c Ask another student / my teacher for help.

To revise go to ...
Student's Book Review >> p.25   Grammar Bank >> p.137
Workbook >> pp.10–13   www.oup.com/elt/result

Reading

Read this text again.
>> **Workbook** >> p.14 exercise 8

How confident are you?
I can understand ...
☐ some words
☐ with help
☐ when I read again
☐ everything

Listening

Listen to this audio again.
Workbook >> p.14 audio script **2S.1▶**
Workbook >> p.14 audio script **2S.2▶**

How confident are you?
I can understand ...
☐ some words
☐ with help
☐ when I listen again
☐ everything

Writing

Do this writing exercise again.
Workbook >> p.15 exercise 13

How confident are you?
I can write ...
☐ with help
☐ on my own
☐ with some mistakes
☐ with no mistakes

What are you going to do now?
a Nothing. I'm happy.
b Ask my teacher for help.
c Practise my reading / listening / writing.

To practise go to ...
Student's Book >> pp.16–24
Workbook >> pp.14–15
MultiRom Listening section
www.oup.com/elt/result

Unit 3 Self check

Grammar

1 Complete the text with the correct form of the verbs in brackets.

I ¹_____ (be) from Turkey. The capital of Turkey ²_____ (be) Ankara but I ³_____ (live) in Trabzon. Our currency ⁴_____ (be) the Turkish lira. My first language ⁵_____ (be) Turkish but I ⁶_____ (speak) German very well.

2 Complete the text with *a*, *an*, or *the*.

I'm Polish and I live in Poland. ¹_____ capital city is Warsaw but I live in ²_____ town called Nowe Miasto. It's near Warsaw. In Poland ³_____ currency is ⁴_____ złoty. ⁵_____ main language is Polish but I speak Russian very well too. I also speak ⁶_____ little English and ⁷_____ little French.

Vocabulary

3 Complete the sentences.
1 The language and nationality of the people from Turkey is _____.
2 The _____ of Russia is Moscow.
3 The nationality of the people from China is _____.
4 The _____ of Germany is the euro.
5 Washington is the capital of _____ USA.

4 Correct the spelling mistakes.
1 I speak Portugese.
2 I speak France and a little German.
3 I'm Brasilian and I live in São Paulo.
4 The nationality of the people from Peru is Peruian.
5 Berlin is the capitel of Germany.

Pronunciation

5 Read the texts aloud. Put the underlined words in the correct box.

●•	●
toilets	

A Excuse me, where are the <u>toilets</u>, please?
B They're over there near <u>platform</u> 12.

A Excuse me, where's the <u>pub</u>, please?
B It's upstairs, near the <u>chemist's</u>.

A Excuse me, where are the <u>taxis</u>, please?
B Taxis? They're near the Fairfield Street <u>exit</u>.

A Excuse me, is this the <u>train</u> to London?
B Sorry, I don't know.

Check your answers on ≫ p.88.

What are you going to do now?
a Nothing. I'm happy.
b Revise grammar / vocabulary / pronunciation and try again.
c Ask another student / my teacher for help.

To revise go to …
Student's Book Review ≫ p.35   Grammar Bank ≫ p.138
Workbook ≫ pp.16–19   **www.oup.com/elt/result**

Reading

Read these texts again.
   Workbook ≫ p.20 exercise 6
   Workbook ≫ p.21 exercise 7

How confident are you?
I can understand …
   ☐ some words
   ☐ with help
   ☐ when I read again
   ☐ everything

Listening

Listen to this audio again.
   Workbook ≫ p.20 audio script **3S.1▶**

How confident are you?
I can understand …
   ☐ some words
   ☐ with help
   ☐ when I listen again
   ☐ everything

Writing

Do this writing exercise again.
   Workbook ≫ p.21 exercise 12

How confident are you?
I can write …
   ☐ with help
   ☐ on my own
   ☐ with some mistakes
   ☐ with no mistakes

What are you going to do now?
   a Nothing. I'm happy.
   b Ask my teacher for help.
   c Practise my reading / listening / writing.

To practise go to …
Student's Book ≫ pp.26–34
Workbook ≫ pp.20–21
MultiRom Listening section
www.oup.com/elt/result

Unit 4 Self check

Grammar

1 Tick ✓ or correct the sentences.

  1 He doesn't works at weekends.

  2 Does you work in a bank?

  3 She doesn't go for a run.

  4 She gets dressed and brush her teeth.

  5 He finishs work at five.

  6 Does she works at weekends?

2 Correct the underlined words.

In Ethiopia we usually get up [1]in six o'clock in the morning and go to bed [2]on nine or ten o'clock [3]of the evening. We have our main meal [4]on about half past twelve. We often have a small meal [5]in six o'clock [6]at the evening.

Vocabulary

3 Complete the sentences with a suitable word.

  1 We u_ _ _ _ _ _ _ work nine to five here.

  2 You a_ _ _ _ _ _ arrive late.

  3 But I n_ _ _ _ leave late!

  4 How o_ _ _ _ _ do you have coffee breaks?

  5 You s_ _ _ _ _ _ _ _ _ leave at twelve o'clock and come back at two!

4 Complete the sentences with these words.

vacancies out closed cancelled order private

  1 I'm at the airport but my flight's _____!

  2 I want to buy a ticket from the machine but it's out of _____.

  3 I want to stay at the Royal Hotel but there are no _____.

  4 You can't go to the supermarket. It is _____ on Sundays.

  5 Everyone wants to go to the game. The tickets are sold _____.

  6 The sign outside his house says '_____. No entry'.

Pronunciation

5 Say these words aloud and write them in the correct box.

~~live~~ ~~leave~~ sit fifth eat free beach chip thing see

/iː/	/ɪ/
leave	live
_____	_____
_____	_____
_____	_____

Check your answers on >> p.88.

What are you going to do now?

  a Nothing. I'm happy.

  b Revise grammar / vocabulary / pronunciation and try again.

  c Ask another student / my teacher for help.

To revise go to ...

Student's Book Review >> p.45   Grammar Bank >> p.139

Workbook >> pp.22–25   www.oup.com/elt/result

Reading

Read these texts again.

    Workbook >> p.26 exercise 1

    Workbook >> p.27 exercise 7

How confident are you?

I can understand ...

  ☐ some words

  ☐ with help

  ☐ when I read again

  ☐ everything

Listening

Listen to this audio again.

    Workbook >> p.26 audio script **4S.1▶**

How confident are you?

I can understand ...

  ☐ some words

  ☐ with help

  ☐ when I listen again

  ☐ everything

Writing

Do this writing exercise again.

    Workbook >> p.27 exercise 10

How confident are you?

I can write ...

  ☐ with help

  ☐ on my own

  ☐ with some mistakes

  ☐ with no mistakes

What are you going to do now?

  a Nothing. I'm happy.

  b Ask my teacher for help.

  c Practise my reading / listening / writing.

To practise go to ...

Student's Book >> pp.36–44

Workbook >> pp.26–27

MultiRom Listening section

www.oup.com/elt/result

Unit 5 Self check

Grammar

1 Underline the correct words.

1 Does / Has he got brown hair?
2 Anne doesn't / hasn't got a dog.
3 Has / Have you got a pen?
4 I haven't / don't have got any paper.
5 You has / have got a problem.

2 Read the conversation and underline the best words.

A I need a gift for my friend Jane.
B Does she ¹likes / got / like wine?
A No, she ²don't / not like / doesn't.
B Has she got a DVD player?
A No, she ³haven't / hasn't got / hasn't.
B OK, give ⁴she / her / him a DVD player.
A They're very expensive.
B Oh, OK. Does she like animals?
A Yes, she ⁵do / does / has.

Vocabulary

3 Match 1–5 with a–e.

1 ☐ Do you know my girlfriend Kate?
2 ☐ My name's Al. It's
3 ☐ Steven, this
4 ☐ Sorry, what's your
5 ☐ Hi Walter. Do

a is Richard.
b name again?
c you remember me?
d Come and meet her.
e short for Alan.

4 Order the words to make sentences and questions.

1 has small eyes grey she .
2 Eric got cat big black has a .
3 an car old red he drives .
4 blonde woman know you the tall do ?
5 got hair dark Frank has long .

Pronunciation

5 Write the words in the correct box.

compl<u>e</u>te wr<u>i</u>te <u>e</u>vening ~~hate~~ n<u>o</u>te ph<u>o</u>ne <u>u</u>se
pl<u>a</u>ce st<u>u</u>dent w<u>i</u>ne

/eɪ/	/iː/	/aɪ/	/əʊ/	/juː/
hate				

Check your answers on >> p.89.

What are you going to do now?

a Nothing. I'm happy.
b Revise grammar / vocabulary / pronunciation and try again.
c Ask another student / my teacher for help.

To revise go to …
Student's Book Review >> p.55   Grammar Bank >> p.140
Workbook >> pp.28–31   **www.oup.com/elt/result**

Reading

Read these texts again.
   Workbook >> p.32 exercise 1
   Workbook >> p.33 exercise 7

How confident are you?
I can understand …
   ☐ some words
   ☐ with help
   ☐ when I read again
   ☐ everything

Listening

Listen to this audio again.
   Workbook >> p.32 audio script **5S.1▶**

How confident are you?
I can understand …
   ☐ some words
   ☐ with help
   ☐ when I listen again
   ☐ everything

Writing

Do this writing exercise again.
   Workbook >> p.33 exercise 11

How confident are you?
I can write …
   ☐ with help
   ☐ on my own
   ☐ with some mistakes
   ☐ with no mistakes

What are you going to do now?
   a Nothing. I'm happy.
   b Ask my teacher for help.
   c Practise my reading / listening / writing.

To practise go to …
Student's Book >> pp.46–54
Workbook >> pp.32–33
MultiRom Listening section
www.oup.com/elt/result

Unit 6 Self check

Grammar

1 <u>Underline</u> the correct words.

Iris Oh dear, I haven't got many tea bags. Have you got ¹any / much?

Sue Yes. How ²much / many do you need?

Iris Two. No, nine or ten ... some for later! ... This is your milk, is that OK? I haven't got ³some / any.

Sue OK. Help yourself!

Iris Oh, there isn't much ... Oops, there isn't any for you, sorry! ... How ⁴much / many sugar do you want? I don't take sugar in tea. Do you?

Sue Well, ehm ...

Iris No, of course you don't. I'd like a biscuit. Have you got ⁵a / any?

Sue Yes, I've got ⁶a / some lot of biscuits, but they're ...

Iris Oh great. Thanks! ... These biscuits are delicious!

2 Write the words in the correct box.

~~egg~~ computer cup coffee CD milk sugar mobile biscuit cheese jam onion bread steak meat

Countable	egg
Uncountable	

Vocabulary

3 Complete these sentences with the correct word.

1 For b_____, a lot of people go to the bars to drink orange juice or coffee with milk, and eat small cakes.

2 They don't drink much t_____, and they never drink it with milk.

3 Don't go for l_____ before two o'clock – you can't get the 'menu of the day' before that.

4 The first c_____ is soup, salad or vegetables.

5 The evening m_____ is at nine or ten o'clock.

4 Correct the spelling mistakes.

1 Are there any potatos in a Russian salad?

2 Are there any carots?

3 I would like a cheese sandwiche.

4 We need appels and bananas.

5 Would you like a biscit with your coffee?

Pronunciation

5 <u>Underline</u> the /ə/ sound.

yog<u>u</u>rt potato supermarket tomato salad sugar

Check your answers on >> p.89.

What are you going to do now?

a Nothing. I'm happy.

b Revise grammar / vocabulary / pronunciation and try again.

c Ask another student / my teacher for help.

To revise go to ...

Student's Book Review >> p.65 Grammar Bank >> p.141

Workbook >> pp.34–37 www.oup.com/elt/result

Reading

Read this text again.

Workbook >> p.38 exercise 2

How confident are you?

I can understand ...

☐ some words

☐ with help

☐ when I read again

☐ everything

Listening

Listen to this audio again.

Workbook >> p.39 audio script **6S.1▶**

How confident are you?

I can understand ...

☐ some words

☐ with help

☐ when I listen again

☐ everything

Writing

Do this writing exercise again.

Workbook >> p.39 exercise 10

How confident are you?

I can write ...

☐ with help

☐ on my own

☐ with some mistakes

☐ with no mistakes

What are you going to do now?

a Nothing. I'm happy.

b Ask my teacher for help.

c Practise my reading / listening / writing.

To practise go to ...

Student's Book >> pp.56–64

Workbook >> pp.38–39

MultiRom Listening section

www.oup.com/elt/result

Unit 7 Self check

Grammar

1 Tick ✓ or correct the sentences.

1 My problem is I can't swimming.
2 Do you go for a run in the morning?
3 What time do you having lunch?
4 I enjoy watch football on TV.
5 She can to swim very quickly.
6 Tom can do it easy.
7 Gary likes having long hair.

2 Underline the correct words.

1 What shall / are we do?
2 Let's / Let go out.
3 Shall / How about going to the cinema?
4 How about / Let's going to the shops?
5 Let's ask / asking William to come to the party.

Vocabulary

3 Complete the sentences with the correct form of *go* or *play*.

1 I always _____ fishing on Sunday morning.
2 Do you enjoy _____ cards?
3 Let's _____ roller-skating this afternoon.
4 Every summer they _____ sailing in the Mediterranean.
5 I love _____ basketball!
6 I want to _____ the guitar.

4 Complete the sentences with these words.

windy   wet   snowy   icy   dry   cloudy

1 The weather is very hot and _____. My flowers need water.
2 It's very _____ today – perfect for skiing!
3 Be careful if you go roller-skating. The roads are very _____.
4 It's very _____ in England – it rains all the time.
5 It's not a good day for golf because it's very _____.
6 You can't see the sun today because it's very _____.

Pronunciation

5 Underline the stressed syllable in each word.

average   photograph
exercise   director
gardening   typical
piano   newspaper

Check your answers on >> p.89.

What are you going to do now?

a Nothing. I'm happy.
b Revise grammar / vocabulary / pronunciation and try again.
c Ask another student / my teacher for help.

To revise go to ...
Student's Book Review >> p.75   Grammar Bank >> p.142
Workbook >> pp.40–43   **www.oup.com/elt/result**

Reading

Read these texts again.

Workbook >> p.44 exercise 4
Workbook >> p.45 exercise 6

How confident are you?
I can understand ...

☐ some words
☐ with help
☐ when I read again
☐ everything

Listening

Listen to this audio again.

Workbook >> p.44 audio script **7S.1▶**

How confident are you?
I can understand ...

☐ some words
☐ with help
☐ when I listen again
☐ everything

Writing

Do this writing exercise again.

Workbook >> p.45 exercise 10

How confident are you?
I can write ...

☐ with help
☐ on my own
☐ with some mistakes
☐ with no mistakes

What are you going to do now?

a Nothing. I'm happy.
b Ask my teacher for help.
c Practise my reading / listening / writing.

To practise go to ...
Student's Book >> pp.66–74
Workbook >> pp.44–45
MultiRom Listening section
www.oup.com/elt/result

Unit 8 Self check

Grammar

1 <u>Underline</u> the best words.

Gene Hackman is Harry Caul, a spy. He [1]watching / watches people. He [2]is listening / listens to their conversations and makes tapes. He [3]isn't understanding / doesn't understand the conversations – they aren't his problem.

One day, Harry is listening to a conversation. The people [4]are talking / talk about a murder plan. This is a problem for Harry. He doesn't like murders. But Harry [5]is making / making a mistake. He thinks he is listening to other people, but really *they* [6]are listening / listen to *him*.

2 Order the words to make sentences and questions.

1 the   wearing   is   girl   jeans   blue ?
2 skirts   friends   wearing   are   girl's   the ?
3 the   musicians   are   jackets   wearing ?
4 dictionary   I'm   using   a   not .
5 aren't   they   sandals   their   wearing .

Vocabulary

3 Match 1–5 with a–e.

1 ☐ I'm wearing sandals,   a a suit and tie.
2 ☐ We're going to a wedding   b or a skirt.
3 ☐ At work I wear   c a warm coat and a hat.
4 ☐ I could wear a dress   d so don't wear trainers.
5 ☐ It's very cold. Wear   e not boots.

4 Complete the sentences with these words.

to   on   for   to   about

1 John's listening _____ the radio.
2 We need to think _____ the grammar.
3 Can you sit _____ that chair?
4 I'm going _____ a walk.
5 We're going _____ the gym this afternoon.

Pronunciation

5 Put these words in the correct box.

~~board~~   bird   short   shirt   fur   walk   work   four

/ɔː/	/ɜː/
board	_____
_____	_____
_____	_____

Check your answers on >> p.89.

What are you going to do now?

a Nothing. I'm happy.
b Revise grammar / vocabulary / pronunciation and try again.
c Ask another student / my teacher for help.

To revise go to ...
Student's Book Review >> p.85   Grammar Bank >> p.143
Workbook >> pp.46–49   www.oup.com/elt/result

Reading

Read these texts again.
   Workbook >> p.50 exercise 1
   Workbook >> p.51 exercise 7

How confident are you?
I can understand ...
   ☐ some words
   ☐ with help
   ☐ when I read again
   ☐ everything

Listening

Listen to this audio again.
   Workbook >> p.50 audio script **8S.1**▶

How confident are you?
I can understand ...
   ☐ some words
   ☐ with help
   ☐ when I listen again
   ☐ everything

Writing

Do this writing exercise again.
   Workbook >> p.51 exercise 11

How confident are you?
I can write ...
   ☐ with help
   ☐ on my own
   ☐ with some mistakes
   ☐ with no mistakes

What are you going to do now?
   a Nothing. I'm happy.
   b Ask my teacher for help.
   c Practise my reading / listening / writing.

To practise go to ...
Student's Book >> pp.76–84
Workbook >> pp.50–51
MultiRom Listening section
www.oup.com/elt/result

Grammar

1 Complete the text with the verbs in brackets in the past simple.

I [1]_____ (walk) up the hill to the Nightmare Hotel. I [2]_____ (stop) at the door but I [3]_____ (can not) see the bell. I [4]_____ (knock) and I [5]_____ (wait) in the cold and windy night. I [6]_____ (look) in the window but there [7]_____ (not be) any light.

2 Correct the <u>underlined</u> words.
1 I <u>haved</u> a sandwich for lunch yesterday.
2 The weather <u>were</u> terrible last night.
3 They <u>do</u> the homework last night.
4 He <u>telled</u> me an interesting story.
5 We <u>go</u> to Warsaw last year.

Vocabulary

3 Complete these phrases with the correct word for giving directions.
1 Don't go right, go l_____ at the corner.
2 The bank is o_____ the museum.
3 Walk a_____ the road.
4 Go out o_____ the door and into the street.
5 The post office is n_____ to the museum.

4 <u>Underline</u> the correct words.
A What was the weather like?
B Perfect. It was warm and [1]sunny / clean.
A Where did you stay? A hotel?
B Yeah, a small hotel. Nice and [2]quiet / noisy, with a beautiful garden and a [3]lovely / boring view of the beach and the countryside.
A Was the beach nice?
B Yeah, [4]delicious / beautiful, yeah. And it wasn't [5]crowded / dry.

Pronunciation

5 Put the words in the correct box.

~~asked~~ closed ended looked knocked started stopped waited

1-syllable verb ●	2-syllable verb ● ●
asked	_____
_____	_____
_____	_____
_____	

Check your answers on >> p.89.

What are you going to do now?
a Nothing. I'm happy.
b Revise grammar / vocabulary / pronunciation and try again.
c Ask another student / my teacher for help.

To revise go to ...
Student's Book Review >> p.95   Grammar Bank >> p.144
Workbook >> pp.52–55   www.oup.com/elt/result

Reading

Read these texts again.
Workbook >> p.56 exercise 2
Workbook >> p.57 exercise 8

How confident are you?
I can understand ...
☐ some words
☐ with help
☐ when I read again
☐ everything

Listening

Listen to this audio again.
Workbook >> p.56 audio script **9S.1▶**

How confident are you?
I can understand ...
☐ some words
☐ with help
☐ when I listen again
☐ everything

Writing

Do this writing exercise again.
Workbook >> p.57 exercise 13

How confident are you?
I can write ...
☐ with help
☐ on my own
☐ with some mistakes
☐ with no mistakes

What are you going to do now?
a Nothing. I'm happy.
b Ask my teacher for help.
c Practise my reading / listening / writing.

To practise go to ...
Student's Book >> pp.86–94
Workbook >> pp.56–57
MultiRom Listening section
www.oup.com/elt/result

Unit 10 Self check

Grammar

1 Underline the correct words.
1 Did you go / went out last Friday?
2 Did / Were you work on Saturday?
3 Ernie didn't have / had a son.
4 Ernie get / got married when he was forty.
5 We didn't / weren't sell the car.

2 Write past simple questions about Pablo Neruda.
1 Where / Pablo Neruda / born

_____?

2 What / real name

_____?

3 Where / go to live

_____?

4 When / write his first poem

_____?

5 When / win the Nobel Prize for Literature

_____?

Vocabulary

3 Match 1–5 with a–e.
1 ☐ I got married   a and studied German.
2 ☐ I became a doctor   b and went to university.
3 ☐ He went to university   c and had a child.
4 ☐ She left school in 2001   d and worked in many countries.
5 ☐ He became a diplomat   e and got a job in a hospital.

4 Write the years.

1800 *eighteen hundred*

1919 _____   1999 _____

1984 _____   2012 _____

2008 _____   1933 _____

Pronunciation

5 Do the underlined letters make a /s/ or a /z/ sound? Write the words in the correct box.

~~news~~ facts his place studies was this quiz

/s/	_____ _____ _____
/z/	*news* _____ _____ _____ _____

Check your answers on >> p.89.

What are you going to do now?
a Nothing. I'm happy.
b Revise grammar / vocabulary / pronunciation and try again.
c Ask another student / my teacher for help.

To revise go to ...
Student's Book Review >> p.105   Grammar Bank >> p.145
Workbook >> pp.58–61   www.oup.com/elt/result

Reading

Read these texts again.
Workbook >> p.62 exercise 1
Workbook >> p.63 exercise 8

How confident are you?
I can understand ...
☐ some words
☐ with help
☐ when I read again
☐ everything

Listening

Listen to this audio again.
Workbook >> p.62 audio script **10S.1▶**

How confident are you?
I can understand ...
☐ some words
☐ with help
☐ when I listen again
☐ everything

Writing

Do this writing exercise again.
Workbook >> p.63 exercise 14

How confident are you?
I can write ...
☐ with help
☐ on my own
☐ with some mistakes
☐ with no mistakes

What are you going to do now?
a Nothing. I'm happy.
b Ask my teacher for help.
c Practise my reading / listening / writing.

To practise go to ...
Student's Book >> pp.96–104
Workbook >> pp.62–63
MultiRom Listening section
www.oup.com/elt/result

Unit 11 Self check

Grammar

1 Write *enough* in each sentence below.
1 The water isn't warm for swimming.
2 He is 1 m 80. The bed isn't big for him.
3 I'm not rich to live in central London!
4 There aren't chairs in the TV room.
5 Oh no! I don't have cups for everyone!

2 Underline the correct words.
1 Ricky's bed is longest / longer than Frank's.
2 The chair is more expensive / expensive than the sofa.
3 This holiday is worse / badder than our holiday last year.
4 That desk is the ugliest / uglier in the shop.
5 What is the warmest / most warm country in Europe?

Vocabulary

3 Match 1–5 with a–e.
1 ☐ You stay for the night and only have breakfast
2 ☐ You have a flat and you cook and clean
3 ☐ You sleep outside
4 ☐ A campsite is a place
5 ☐ The five-star hotel has

a in a tent.
b in a self-catering apartment.
c where people put their tents.
d a bar, pool, and restaurants.
e in a bed and breakfast.

4 Complete the sentences with these words.

lift washbasin hand-made antique shelf

1 I need a _____ for my books.
2 There is a small _____ in the bathroom.
3 This _____ table is two hundred years old.
4 The chairs were _____ by my father. He loved making things.
5 We have to walk up the stairs because the _____ is broken.

Pronunciation

5 Underline the stressed syllable in each word.

attractive   fantastic   friendly
comfortable   beautiful   modern
excellent   delicious   ugly

Check your answers on >> p.90.

What are you going to do now?
a Nothing. I'm happy.
b Revise grammar / vocabulary / pronunciation and try again.
c Ask another student / my teacher for help.

To revise go to ...
Student's Book Review >> p.115   Grammar Bank >> p.146
Workbook >> pp.64–67   www.oup.com/elt/result

Reading

Read this text again.
Workbook >> p.68 exercise 1

How confident are you?
I can understand ...
☐ some words
☐ with help
☐ when I read again
☐ everything

Listening

Listen to this audio again.
Workbook >> p.69 audio script 11S.1▶

How confident are you?
I can understand ...
☐ some words
☐ with help
☐ when I listen again
☐ everything

Writing

Do this writing exercise again.
Workbook >> p.69 exercise 13

How confident are you?
I can write ...
☐ with help
☐ on my own
☐ with some mistakes
☐ with no mistakes

What are you going to do now?
a Nothing. I'm happy.
b Ask my teacher for help.
c Practise my reading / listening / writing.

To practise go to ...
Student's Book >> pp.106–114
Workbook >> pp.68–69
MultiRom Listening section
www.oup.com/elt/result

Unit 12 Self check

Grammar

1 Write the complete questions. Use the present continuous.

1 When / Justin / take a day off sick?
2 What / you / do on Friday?
3 How / you / get there?
4 Where / you / stay?
5 Where / you / go this evening?
6 Who / you / see tonight?

2 Order the words to make sentences.

1 at two sister meeting my o'clock I'm .
2 I'm Tony tennis tonight playing with .
3 next learn going German I'm to year .
4 quit to I'm smoking going .
5 Ana tomorrow lunch with I'm having .

Vocabulary

3 Complete the sentences with these words.

weekdays afternoon thing day evening

1 His appointment is late tomorrow _____, at 5.30.
2 The appointment is at 10.45 the _____ after tomorrow.
3 I'm going to the bank first _____ tomorrow. At 8 a.m.
4 We're meeting in a café at 8.00 this _____.
5 She starts work at 9.00 on _____ and 10.00 at weekends.

4 Underline the correct words.

1 I don't feel good / well.
2 I think I'm / it's flu.
3 I'm going to phone in ill / sick.
4 He's going to take / make a day off work.
5 Mary's not in the office because she's on sick leave / holiday.

Pronunciation

5 Match the words with the sounds.

1 ☐ feel   a /æ/
2 ☐ fill   b /e/
3 ☐ fun   c /əʊ/
4 ☐ hat   d /ɑː/
5 ☐ heart   e /eɪ/
6 ☐ not   f /iː/
7 ☐ note   g /ɪ/
8 ☐ pain   h /ʌ/
9 ☐ pen   i /ɒ/

Check your answers on >> p.90.

What are you going to do now?

a Nothing. I'm happy.
b Revise grammar / vocabulary / pronunciation and try again.
c Ask another student / my teacher for help.

To revise go to ...
Student's Book Review >> p.125   Grammar Bank >> p.147
Workbook >> pp.70–73   www.oup.com/elt/result

Reading

Read these texts again.

Workbook >> p.74 exercise 5
Workbook >> p.75 exercise 6

How confident are you?
I can understand ...

☐ some words
☐ with help
☐ when I read again
☐ everything

Listening

Listen to this audio again.

Workbook >> p.74 audio script **12S.1**▶

How confident are you?
I can understand ...

☐ some words
☐ with help
☐ when I listen again
☐ everything

Writing

Do this writing exercise again.

Workbook >> p.75 exercise 10

How confident are you?
I can write ...

☐ with help
☐ on my own
☐ with some mistakes
☐ with no mistakes

What are you going to do now?

a Nothing. I'm happy.
b Ask my teacher for help.
c Practise my reading / listening / writing.

To practise go to ...
Student's Book >> pp.116–124
Workbook >> pp.74–75
MultiRom Listening section
www.oup.com/elt/result

Self checks answer key

Unit 1
Grammar
1
1 name's
2 I'm
3 is
4 My
5 is
6 My
7 number's

2
1 is
2 you
3 What's
4 How
5 your

Vocabulary
3
1 eleven
2 three
3 seventeen
4 eight
5 nineteen
6 fifty-five
7 seventy-six
8 twelve

4
1 Excuse me, what's your name?
2 His email address is jim@teleline.uk.
3 Thanks for the coffee.
4 How do you spell it?
5 My phone number is 91 456 2110.

Pronunciation
5 a, j, k
m, f, l, n
t, v, b, d
y, i

Unit 2
Grammar
1 Hi! My name's Max. I'm from Canada. I'm eighteen years old and I live with my parents. My mother's name's Sara and she's a doctor. My father's name's Jed and he's a driver.

2
1 Their
2 His
3 Our
4 your
5 her
6 My

Vocabulary
3
1 young
2 married
3 rich
4 old
5 divorced
6 single

4
1 half
2 quarter
3 ten
4 twenty
5 midnight

Pronunciation
5
1 thirty
2 fifty
3 sixteen
4 ninety
5 nineteen
6 seventeen
7 forty
8 fourteen

Unit 3
Grammar
1
1 am/'m
2 is/'s
3 live
4 is/'s
5 is
6 speak

2
1 The
2 a
3 the
4 the
5 The
6 a
7 a

Vocabulary
3
1 Turkish
2 capital
3 Chinese
4 currency
5 the

4
1 I speak **Portuguese**.
2 I speak **French** and a little German.
3 I'm **Brazilian** and I live in São Paulo.
4 The nationality of the people from Peru is **Peruvian**.
5 Berlin is the **capital** of Germany.

Pronunciation
5 ●● toilets, platform, chemist's, taxis, exit
● pub, train

Unit 4
Grammar
1
1 He doesn't work at weekends.
2 Do you work in a bank?
3 ✓
4 She gets dressed and brushes her teeth.
5 He finishes work at five.
6 Does she work at weekends?

2
1 at
2 at
3 in
4 at
5 at
6 in

Vocabulary
3
1 usually
2 always
3 never
4 often
5 sometimes

4
1 cancelled
2 order
3 vacancies
4 closed
5 out
6 Private

Pronunciation
5 /iː/ leave, eat, free, beach, see
/ɪ/ live, sit, fifth, chip, thing

Unit 5
Grammar
1
1 Has
2 hasn't
3 Have
4 haven't
5 have

2
1 like
2 doesn't
3 hasn't
4 her
5 does

Vocabulary
3
1 d
2 e
3 a
4 b
5 c

4
1 She has small grey eyes.
2 Eric has got a big black cat.
3 He drives an old red car.
4 Do you know the tall blonde woman?
5 Frank has got long dark hair.

Pronunciation

5 /eɪ/ hate, place
/iː/ complete, evening
/aɪ/ write, wine
/əʊ/ note, phone
/juː/ use, student

Unit 6

Grammar

1 1 any
2 many
3 any
4 much
5 any
6 a

2 Countable: egg, computer, cup, CD,
mobile, biscuit, onion, steak
Uncountable: coffee, milk, sugar,
cheese, jam, bread, meat

Vocabulary

3 1 breakfast
2 tea
3 lunch
4 course
5 meal

4 1 Are there any **potatoes** in a Russian salad?
2 Are there any **carrots**?
3 I would like a cheese **sandwich**.
4 We need **apples** and bananas.
5 Would you like a **biscuit** with your coffee?

Pronunciation

5 yog<u>u</u>rt
pot<u>a</u>to
sup<u>er</u>market
tom<u>a</u>to
sala<u>d</u>
sug<u>a</u>r

Unit 7

Grammar

1 1 My problem is I can't swim.
2 ✓
3 What time do you have lunch?
4 I enjoy watching football on TV.
5 She can swim very quickly.
6 Tom can do it easily.
7 ✓

2 1 shall
2 Let's
3 How about
4 How about
5 ask

Vocabulary

3 1 go
2 playing
3 go
4 go
5 playing
6 play

4 1 dry
2 snowy
3 icy
4 wet
5 windy
6 cloudy

Pronunciation

5 <u>a</u>verage
<u>e</u>xercise
<u>gar</u>dening
<u>pi</u>ano
<u>pho</u>tograph
<u>di</u>rector
<u>ty</u>pical
<u>new</u>spaper

Unit 8

Grammar

1 1 watches
2 listens
3 doesn't understand
4 are talking
5 is making
6 are listening

2 1 Is the girl wearing blue jeans?
2 Are the girl's friends wearing skirts?
3 Are the musicians wearing jackets?
4 I'm not using a dictionary.
5 They aren't wearing their sandals.

Vocabulary

3 1 e
2 d
3 a
4 b
5 c

4 1 to
2 about
3 on
4 for
5 to

Pronunciation

5 /ɔː/ board, short, walk, four
/ɜː/ bird, shirt, fur, work

Unit 9

Grammar

1 1 walked
2 stopped
3 couldn't
4 knocked
5 waited
6 looked
7 wasn't

2 1 had
2 was
3 did
4 told
5 went

Vocabulary

3 1 left
2 opposite
3 across
4 of
5 next

4 1 sunny
2 quiet
3 lovely
4 beautiful
5 crowded

Pronunciation

5 ● asked, closed, looked, knocked, stopped
●● ended, started, waited

Unit 10

Grammar

1 1 go
2 Did
3 have
4 got
5 didn't

2 1 Where was Pablo Neruda born?
2 What was his real name?
3 Where did he go to live?
4 When did he write his first poem?
5 When did he win the Nobel Prize for Literature?

Vocabulary

3 1 c
2 e
3 a
4 b
5 d

Self checks answer key

4 1919 nineteen nineteen
1984 nineteen eighty-four
2008 two thousand and eight
1999 nineteen ninety-nine
2012 two thousand and twelve
1933 nineteen thirty-three

Pronunciation
5 /s/ fact<u>s</u>, pla<u>ce</u>, thi<u>s</u>
/z/ new<u>s</u>, hi<u>s</u>, studie<u>s</u>, wa<u>s</u>, qui<u>z</u>

Unit 11

Grammar
1 1 The water isn't warm enough for swimming.
2 He is 1 m 80. The bed isn't big enough for him.
3 I'm not rich enough to live in central London!
4 There aren't enough chairs in the TV room.
5 Oh no! I don't have enough cups for everyone!

2 1 longer
2 more expensive
3 worse
4 ugliest
5 warmest

Vocabulary
3 1 e
2 b
3 a
4 c
5 d

4 1 shelf
2 washbasin
3 antique
4 hand-made
5 lift

Pronunciation
5 att<u>ra</u>ctive
<u>com</u>fortable
<u>ex</u>cellent
fant<u>a</u>stic
be<u>au</u>tiful
de<u>li</u>cious
<u>frien</u>dly
<u>mo</u>dern
<u>ug</u>ly

Unit 12

Grammar
1 1 When is Justin taking a day off sick?
2 What are you doing on Friday?
3 How are you getting there?
4 Where are you staying?
5 Where are you going this evening?
6 Who are you seeing tonight?

2 1 I'm meeting my sister at two o'clock.
2 I'm playing tennis with Tony tonight.
3 I'm going to learn German next year.
4 I'm going to quit smoking.
5 I'm having lunch with Ana tomorrow.

Vocabulary
3 1 afternoon
2 day
3 thing
4 evening
5 weekdays

4 1 well
2 it's
3 sick
4 take
5 leave

Pronunciation
5 1 f
2 g
3 h
4 a
5 d
6 i
7 c
8 e
9 b

Audio scripts

1

1A.1
A Hello, good **mor**ning! **What's** your **name**?
B Hello, good **mor**ning! **My** name's **Jane**.
A **Nice** to **meet** you! **My** name's **Drew**.
B Hello, **Drew**! **Nice** to meet **you**!

1B.1
Phone numbers
384 6652
499 7411
406 5889
221 3075

Email addresses
iou2o@busby.net
okchen@vanzine.int
quick4@spt.com
lin3@lovebird.org

Websites
www.boptunes.esl
www.ugetwell.co.uk
www.digipix.net
www.readit.net

1C.1
What's your **first** name? Claire.
What's your **sur**name? Palmer.
How do you **spell** that? P-A-L-M-E-R.
Where are you **from**? Canada.
What's your ad**dress**? 42 Ashford Street, Toronto.

1S.1
1 A Good morning, sir. Your name please?
  B Marwan Raharjo.
  A **How do you spell your surname?**
  B R-A, H-A-R, J-O.
  A R-A, H-A-R, J-O. Thank you. And your age?
  B I'm thirty-five.
  A Forty-five?
  B No, thirty-five.
  A And where are you from?
  B Holland.
  A H-O, double L, A-N-D. Thank you. And your email? Do you have an email address?
  B Yes, it's, er, marwara@belanda.net. That's M-A-R, W-A-R-A at B-E-L, A-N-D-A.
  A B-E-L, A-N-D-A.
  B Yes, that's right. Dot net.
  A Dot net. Right! Thank you, sir.
2 A Good evening! Miss van der Post?
  B Yes?
  A This is hotel reception speaking. I'm sorry, but I can't read your writing on the form. Could I just check your details?
  B Yes, of course.
  A Thank you. Could you tell me your first name?

B Gillian.
A Erm, is that with a J or a G?
B With a G. G-I, double L, I-A-N.
A G-I, double L, I-A-N. And your marital status?
B **Sorry?**
A Are you married?
B Oh no, no I'm not. I'm single.
A **Two more questions.** What's your phone number?
B 976 343 918.
A 9-7-6, 3-4, 3-9, 1-8. And your passport number?
B My passport number. Just a moment. Ah yes: SA – 500255.
A SA – 5 double 0, 2 double 5. Thank you very much.
B You're welcome.
3 A Now, Mr Collins, **four more questions, please.** What's your first name?
  B Sean.
  A **Could you spell that for me?**
  B S-E-A-N.
  A S-E-A-N. OK. Age?
  B **Can you just repeat that?**
  A Your age. How old are you?
  B Ah! I'm 31.
  A Thirty-one. And your marital status?
  B Married.
  A Right – married. And question number four – what's your passport number?
  B I don't remember. You have my passport!
  A Oh yes, you're right – here it is! Erm, it's er RI-2273168! RI, double 2 7, 3-1, 6-8. Thank you.

2

2A.1
2-syllable words: question, Monday, Wednesday, answer, evening, English, weekend, Thursday

3-syllable words: afternoon, underline, umbrella, Saturday

2C.1
His girlfriend is an English teacher.
Her parents are designers.
She's an engineer.
The shop assistant is sixteen years old.
My boyfriend is a good actor.

2D.1
1 It's half past six.
2 It's quarter to ten.
3 It's two thirty.
4 It's ten to eight.
5 It's twenty past four.
6 It's about five o'clock, um, yes, five to five.

2D.2
Is it on TV1? No, it's on TV**2**.
Is it on Monday morning?
No, it's on Monday **evening**.
Is it on Tuesday morning?
No, it's on **Monday** morning.
Is it at six o'clock?
No, it's at **twelve** o'clock.
Is it at ten past eight?
No, it's at **twenty** past eight.
Is it at five to nine?
No, it's at five to **ten**.
Is it the news?
No, it's the **football**.

2S.1
1 This is a recorded message. Doctor Watson's office **is closed at** the moment. The doctor is available on Tuesday **and Thursday evenings**, from six o'clock to nine o'clock. That's Tuesday and Thursday evenings from six to nine.
2 Hello. Sorry, but we are now closed. The office is open from Tuesday to Friday, in the mornings, between half-past nine and half-past two. That's Tuesday to Friday, 9.30 to 2.30. Thank you.
3 This is a recorded message. Thank you for calling. Please call again in shop opening times. The shop is open every day Monday to Saturday, nine o'clock to half-past four in the afternoon. Thank you.
4 This is Bristol Street Primary School. Sorry, but the school is closed at the moment. Please call later. The school is open every day, Monday to Friday, from 8.30 in the morning to 4.30 in the afternoon. That's 8.30 to 4.30. Thank you.

2S.2
1 Hi, my name's Eric. I'm from France. I'm **25 years old**, and I'm single. I live with my parents. And my job? Well, **I'm a designer**.
2 This is my girlfriend, Maria. No, **not my wife** – my girlfriend! She's 23, she's from Italy, and she's **a shop assistant**.
3 These two are my friends from university. They're **a married couple**. Their names are Annie and Paul. They have no children. He's an engineer, a computer engineer, and she's a school teacher, a **primary school teacher**.
4 This is Françoise. She's 37 and **she's divorced**. She has two children: a young boy of six and a girl of sixteen. **She isn't rich**. She's an office worker.

5 **These are friends** who live in Switzerland. His name is Klaus and her name is Louise. **They aren't married**. She's 22 years old and a university student. He's about 30, and he's a doctor at the local hospital.

3

3A.1
Is this the train to Manchester?
No, that train's on platform 4.

Excuse me! Where are the telephones?
They're over there, near the exit.

Where's the café, please?
It's upstairs, near the music shop.

Excuse me, is this the car park?
No, it isn't. It's over there, near the chemist's.

Excuse me, where are the cash machines, please?
They're near the bookshop.

3B.1
Portugal
Portuguese
Egypt
Egyptian
Japan
Japanese
China
Chinese

3C.1
house   houses
school   schools
watch   watches
shop   shops
church   churches
glass   glasses
street   streets
girl   girls
town   towns

3S.1
A Excuse me. **Is there a bus stop near here?**
B A bus stop? Yes, madam. It's just outside.
A Can you show me on the map?
B Yes, of course. A5, that's it there.
A A5?
B That's right.
A Thank you very much.

A Sorry?
B Yes?
A I need some cash, and I can't find any cash machines.
B Oh. Well, er, **look, the cash machines are there**, erm, A14.
A Oh I see. A14. Thanks!

A Excuse me.
B Yes?
A I can't see the map properly, and **I don't have my glasses with me**. Could you tell me where the toilets are?

B The toilets? Erm, that's them right there – A8.
A Eighty-eight?
B No, A – 8, near the supermarket.
A Oh, sorry! A8. Thank you very much.

A Excuse me! I'm looking for the South Street exit.
B Oh yes. That's, er, A2, **at the other end of the shopping centre**. Near the toilets.
A A2? Thanks.

A Sorry?
B Yes?
A Do you know if there's a chemist's here?
B Erm, just a moment. Let's have a look at the map. Chemist's. **Oh yes, here it is**! A7, next to the bookshop.
A A7, next to the bookshop. Thanks!

4

4A.1
The football's on in five minutes but the TV is out of order. – Oh no!

I'm at the supermarket and everything is half-price today. – That's great!

My car! My car! It's not in the car park! – Oh no!

We have a new car! – Oh really?

My sister has a new baby. – That's great!

We get married on Monday! – Good luck!

My father's in bed. – Oh really?

My cat isn't very well. – I'm sorry!

School is closed today. – That's great!

It's 9.30 and my exam's at ten o'clock. – Good luck!

4B.1
1 the seventh of April
2 the fifteenth of April
3 the fourth of August
4 the twentieth of August
5 the third of October
6 the ninth of October

4C.1
He wakes up early.
She gets up late.
He checks the mail.

She goes for a run.
He has fruit for breakfast.
She leaves the house.

He watches TV.
She brushes her teeth.
He finishes work.

4S.1
A So, Jack, you're a lorry driver. Tell me **about your** normal week.
J Normal week? **I don't have** any normal weeks! Yeah, well, I usually work **Monday to Friday**, but, erm, it's often **weekends** too. I mean, for example, I live in France, you know, and, er, on Monday I drive to Holland for a container, and I take, take that to Germany.
A And how long is the trip?
J About a day, I suppose, yeah, a day or so. Anyway, so I'm in Holland on Monday, then, er, I sleep in Germany on Tuesday night, you know, and then on Wednesday, er, I go from Germany to the north of Italy.
A So when do you arrive in Italy?
J If I'm lucky, I get there on Wednesday night, but it all depends, you know, the traffic, the weather …
A Yeah, right. And after Italy?
J Well, usually I go up to Austria, you know. That's quite near, so I can relax on Thursday, maybe go for a run in the evening.
A Ah, so you have, er, like a break on Thursdays?
J Yeah, usually. Not always, you know! Sometimes I have to go to another country.
A And Fridays? What do you do on Fridays?
J Well, on Fridays the usual thing is to come back to France, and maybe do a small local job.
A You mean you arrive in France on Friday?
J Normally, yes.
A So your family – what about the family? Do you see them often?
J Maybe on Saturdays and Sundays, when I'm at home in France. But sometimes I'm away from home for two or three weeks, so I don't see them very often.
A So do you like driving your lorry?
J Well! It's not easy. The hours are long and the money isn't so good. It's just a job …

5

5D.1
I've **got** a **bike** but I **haven't got** a **car**.
I've **got** a **clock** but I **want** to get a **watch**.
I've **got** a **cat** but I'd **rather** have a **dog**.
I've **got** a **flat** but I **want** to buy a **house**.
I've **got** a **wife** but she **isn't** very **nice**.
Sorry, dear.

5S.1
a A Mr Patel! **How** are you?
B Fine, thanks, Mike. And you?
A **We're** fine, thank you. Do you know my brother Henry?
B No, I don't think so.
A Come and meet **him**. Henry, this is Mr Patel, **our** neighbour. Mr Patel, Henry, **my brother**.
C Nice to meet you!
B Yes, **you** too.

b A Hello Jenny! Do you remember me?
B Erm, sorry, no, I don't.
A Oh Jenny! My name's Ricardo!
B Ricardo … Just a moment – are you Ricky Marvin?
A Yes, that's right! Ricky Marvin, from school.
B Oh yes, I remember you now. Long blond hair, blue eyes. You've got short hair now, and it's brown.
A Yes. Oh, and this is my wife, Elena.
B Nice to meet you, Elena!

c A Who's that woman over there?
B Where?
A Over there, next to the window. The woman with long brown hair and green eyes.
B Ah, that's Sheila. We work together at the office.
A Oh really?
B Yes. Come and meet her. Sheila, this is my wife, Stella. Stella, this is Sheila.
A&C Nice to meet you!
A Sorry, what's your name again?
C Sheila.
A So you work at the office with Bill?
C Yes, that's right …

6

6A.1
How **much** are the **crisps**?
How **much** is the **wine**?
They're **one** euro **twenty**, and **five** ninety-**nine**.

6C.1
My sister likes an actor,
so she buys him a flower,
she sends him a letter,
but he never sends an answer.

6D.1
some **bread** and **butter**
some **ham** and **eggs**
a **piece** of **pizza**
some **chicken legs**
some **tea** or **coffee**
with **milk** or **sugar**
What would you **like**?
a **glass** of **water**
– please!

6S.1
1 A Is the food all right, madam?
B Yes, thank you. It's fine.
A Would you like any wine?
B Ah, yes, please.
A Red or white?
B Red, please.
A Would you like a bottle or glass?
B Oh, er, a bottle please. A bottle of red wine.
A Thank you, madam.

2 A Hello, Jane. Have you got any crisps?
B Er, yes, I have.

A Oh really? Well, I've got an apple, but I don't like apples.
B So?
A Well, I want some crisps. Can I give you my apple, and you give me the crisps?
B How many do you want?
A How many? Erm, the bag of crisps!
B Oh, OK. Here you are.
A Wow, thanks!
B And my apple?
A Oops, sorry!

3 A Anna! It's lovely to see you.
B It's good to see you too, John.
A Would you like a cup of coffee?
B Yes, please, I'd love one.
A Do you take milk?
B No, thanks.
A Sugar?
B Er, yes, please.
A There are some sandwiches on the table. Butter or jam – help yourself!
B Thank you, that's great.
A So, tell me your news …

4 A Oh, hello Bob. How are you?
B Fine thanks, Jeff. Erm, listen, have you got any eggs?
A Eggs?
B Yeah, my girlfriend's here for lunch, and I haven't got any eggs.
A How many do you want?
B Four would be great!
A OK. Anything else?
B Well, erm, sugar?
A How much sugar do you need?
B A cup of sugar would be great, thanks.
A OK, I won't be a second.
B Thanks very much!

7

7C.1
She can drive a bus,
she can run fast,
and she can understand Spanish,
but she **can't** cook anything,
she **can't** play football,
and she **can't** remember my name!

7D.1
Hello Henry!
house and home
half an hour
Who works hard?
She hates the housework!
When's your holiday?
I need help with my homework!

7S.1
Welcome to the Holiday Out Club! We are open six months a year and offer activities for all different age groups. I'd just like to take a moment to explain the map of the club for you. Number one on your map is the main hotel building – that's the hotel at number one. And, erm, opposite the hotel is the car park. We have spaces for 200 cars, you

know! So, number eleven is the car park. Now, next to that you can see the, er, cinema at number twelve, and the disco at number ten. **Have you got that?** That's the cinema at number twelve, and disco at number ten. Erm, now, let me see, ah yes, next to the hotel we have the shopping centre, that's, er, restaurants at number two, and bars next door at number four – **all right?** The bars at number four, yes. That means the shops are at number three, and the hairdresser's is at number five. **OK?** That brings us to number six, the gym, next to the shopping centre. That's right! That's the gym, with lots of activities, sports, and exercises for everyone! Opposite the gym is the park, **can you see that?** That's number eight, the park. And then next to the park is the swimming pool. Yes, that's number nine, the swimming pool. Finally, on the right, you can see the River Wyle. That's number seven. We use the river for boating and also for swimming. **Any questions?** No? Well, that's all, thank you. We hope you enjoy your stay with us. If you do have any questions, our staff will be very happy to help you …

8

8A.1
A We usually have a snack at about four o'clock.
B It's ten to four now. Let's eat!
A We're going to the football match.
B Oh! I'd love to go to the match!
A We're going for a sandwich. Would you like one?
B I'd like two please! One ham, one cheese.
A We're going for a drink! Would you like to come?
B I'd love to come, but I've got two exams tomorrow – English and maths.

8B.1
I can't find my shirts!
We're going to work this afternoon.
What's that board on the tree?
She lives on the third floor.
Mum! Where are my football shorts?
What time do you start working?
Smith! Is this your bird?
What's the fourth country on the map?

8C.1
something – anything – nothing
reading – writing – speaking
driving a car
walking in the park
riding a bike
making dinner
doing exercises
having a bath
thinking about you

8D.1
We're watching **them**, but **they** aren't watching **us**.
He's looking at **her**, but **she** isn't looking at **him**.
She likes **him**, but **he** doesn't like **her**.
He always phones **her**, but **she** never phones **him**!
We sometimes invite **them**, but **they** don't invite **us**!
She talks about **him**, but **he** doesn't talk about **her**.

8S.1
A Can you hear me all right?
B Yes. I'm in the station. Describe the man for me.
A OK. He's about sixty years old. Yes, sixty. He's **a tall man**, with grey hair – **short grey hair**. He's holding a magazine. No, not a magazine, sorry, a newspaper.
B OK. What's he wearing?
A Um, he's wearing a coat, **a long black coat**. He's not wearing a suit, but he is wearing a shirt and tie. Yes, that's right, a shirt and tie. Maybe **a black tie**.
B Is he carrying anything?
A Yes, I think he's carrying a sweater over his arm.
B Is he wearing glasses?
A No, he's not.
B Hmm … this is difficult. There are lots of men that look the same. What about his shoes?
A Oh! He's wearing **white shoes**, white shoes, now I remember!
B Aha! There he is!

9

9A.1
1 Excuse me, how can I get to the museum, please?
2 Excuse me, how can I get to the museum, please?
3 Excuse me, how can I get to the airport, please?
4 Excuse me, how can I get to the airport, please?
5 Excuse me, how can I get to the hospital, please?
6 Excuse me, how can I get to the hospital, please?
7 Excuse me, how can I get to the park, please?
8 Excuse me, how can I get to the park, please?

9B.1
It's the first left at the corner.
There's a bank at the corner.
The post office is just opposite.
Go straight on and turn left at the lights.
The map says there's an art gallery near here.
It's across the bridge and on the left.
Turn right again into Union Street.
I think there's a tourist information office in the station.

9C.1
4 The beach is nice
The boys are fun
The water is warm
In the holiday sun
But my parents are here
But my parents are here
5 The food was good
The weather was great
The drinks were cheap
The bars opened late
But our daughter was there
But our daughter was there

9D.1
He waited at the bus stop.
It started to rain.
He opened his umbrella.
A voice asked him to help.
He answered her question.
They walked into town.
They talked all the way.
And who knows what happened after that!

9S.1
Well, I went to France **last summer**, on a **cheap holiday**. I stayed in youth hostels, you know, where **you can meet** lots of **young people**, and, er, they tell you all the **good places** to visit. I was travelling alone, I mean, I just wanted a break. The first day I got a cheap flight to Lyon and then travelled west into the mountains. Just fantastic! The real countryside of France! Lots of small towns with their castles and traditions. And then, one day in the middle of France, I met a friend of mine from university! It was incredible! I arrived at this youth hostel, and there was Brian, waiting for the place to open! So we talked and talked about friends and work and family – it was just great! And another day I found this amazing ceramics shop in a little village – you know how I love ceramics – and I spent the day watching this woman make her things. Ah, and I was very lucky with the weather. In the whole three weeks I was there, it only rained twice. I can't wait to go back. It was such a wonderful holiday!

10

10A.1
I met my new boss this morning!
What did you think?
They went to a Thai restaurant.
What did they eat?
My brother phoned.
What did he say?
We went shopping yesterday.
What did you buy?
His children were on TV!
What did they do?
My parents are here.
When did they come?
She went away last summer.
Where did she go?
It's not raining now.
When did it stop?

10B.1
He wrote home.
She rides like an adult.
We sent her a gift for her birthday.
That's Batman!
It's a hard job!
They went down this morning.

10C.1
Tommy was a **wai**ter
Who **didn't** like his **boss**
He **didn't** really **hate** her
But he **didn't** keep his **job**

10D.1
Greenpeace
blue eyes
Police!
Yes, Miss
plays in the theatre
these books

10S.1
A Did you see the film on TV last night?
B No, I didn't. I was studying.
A Poor thing!
B I had an exam this morning! Anyway – what happened?
A This woman had a cat, right?
B OK.
A And there was something wrong with the cat, so she took it to the vet's clinic.
B **And?**
A Well, the cat died.
B Oh no!
A Yes, and then the woman wanted revenge on the vet.
B But vets don't kill animals!
A I know, but she thought the vet was bad and didn't help the cat.
B **So what did she do?**
A Well, she sent him a box of chocolates. Poisoned chocolates. But he didn't eat them.
B **Why not?**
A He didn't like chocolates! He gave them to someone else, and that person nearly died.
B **Didn't she stop then?**
A No, no! The vet wasn't dead, so she didn't stop. She sent him a book with poisoned pages.
B Oh, yeah?
A Yeah, but he didn't like the book, so he didn't even open it.
B No luck with the poison, eh?
A No.
B **So did she kill him in the end?**
A Well, she got really angry and went to the vet's clinic with a gun. She waited at the door, and when the vet came out …
B **She shot him?**
A She tried, but the gun didn't work!
B Lucky for the vet!
A Yeah, so in the end, the police took her away.
B Hmm, shame I missed it …

11

11A.1
adjective
conversation
exercise
information
interview
sentences
syllables
vocabulary

11C.1
Winter sleep
The days become shorter not longer
The weather becomes colder not warmer
Inside is warmer than outside
His eyes become smaller then close
Sleep the winter sleep
Wait for a better life in the spring

11D.1
a bottle of wine
a plate of beans
a piece of paper
a wonderful view
a white bathroom washbasin
we have pink, white, or black shelves

11S.1
A Fairfield Holiday Apartments. Can I help you?
B Er, yes! Yes, you can! My family and I are in apartment number six, and **we have a problem**.
A And what's the problem?
B As a matter of fact, there are several problems.
A Oh dear. What's wrong?
B The fridge doesn't work, the kitchen is dirty, there's no toilet paper, the heating is too hot ...
A Erm, just a moment please. Could you **repeat that more** slowly?
B The fridge doesn't work.
A Yes.
B The kitchen is dirty.
A OK.
B There's no toilet paper.
A I see.
B The temperature's too hot. The heating is too high.
A All right. Anything else?
B There aren't enough towels in the bathroom.
A Uh-huh. Now, erm, could you just give **me your name**?
B Jones, Jonathan Jones.
A Right, Mr Jones. And what time **did you arrive** at the apartment?
B Half-past four this afternoon.
A And what's the **number of your** apartment?
B Number 6. I told you that at the beginning!
A Yes, you did. Well, Mr Jones, you do have a problem!
B I know! I told you that as well! Isn't anybody going to do anything?
A Oh yes, Mr Jones! You're in the wrong apartment. Your reservation is for apartment number 16, not number 6! Didn't you come to reception when you arrived?
B What? Reception? Er, well, yes, I'm sure we did – didn't we?

12

12A.1
1 The dentist's.
2 The dentist's?
3 On Friday morning?
4 On Friday morning.
5 Nine-thirty.
6 Nine-thirty?
7 An hour later.
8 An hour later?
9 For coffee?
10 For coffee.

12C.1
What are you doing next week?
Where are you going?
Who are you meeting?
What are you eating?

When are you going on holiday?
Where are you staying?
What are you doing?
Who are you taking?

12D.1
1 She doesn't want to go.
2 She doesn't wanna go.
3 He's gonna stop smoking.
4 He's going to stop smoking.
5 I wanna leave early today.
6 I want to leave early today.
7 They aren't going to listen to you!
8 They aren't gonna listen to you!

12S.1
1 A Briggs Bank, King Street branch. Can I help you?
B Is that the bank?
A Yes, sir. This is Briggs Bank.
B Erm, **I'd like to make an appointment to speak to the manager, please**.
A **One moment, please ... OK, which day were you thinking of?**
B Er, **some time this week, before the weekend**.
A Would Thursday be all right?
B Did you say Tuesday?
A No, sorry, Thursday!
B Yes, that's fine.
A At eleven in the morning?
B Eleven o'clock?
A Yes.
B That's fine. My name's Brunel.
A **Right, thank you Mr Brunel. That's next Thursday at eleven in the morning.**
B Thursday at eleven o'clock. Fine. Bye!

2 A Baybridge Dentist. Good morning.
B Erm, good morning! Erm, I need to see a dentist.
A Yes. You'd like to make an appointment?
B Please. I've got this terrible toothache.
A I see. When would you like the appointment?
B Oooh, as soon as possible!

A Yes, well, how about seven o'clock this evening?
B Did you say seven o'clock? Is there anything earlier than that?
A Erm, only at 4.15, madam.
B 4.50?
A No, madam – 4.15.
B Ah! All right, er, 4.15 is fine.
A And your name please?
B Johnson, T. Johnson.
A All right, Ms Johnson. We'll expect you today at 4.15.
B Thank you very much!

3 A Good afternoon, Wilson's Mechanic's here.
B Ah, yes, erm, I've got a problem with the car.
A Erm, what's the problem?
B I don't know. The car doesn't work. Could you have a look at it?
A You'll need to make an appointment, I'm afraid. Let me see ... I can give you a time for next week.
B Next week?!
A Yes, madam. Today is Thursday.
B All right. How about Monday?
A Monday ... Monday lunch time, erm, twelve o'clock.
B Twelve o'clock on Monday?
A Yes, madam. Can I have your name, please?
B Erm, Weaver, Jenny Weaver.
A Right, thank you Ms Weaver. We'll see you on Monday.
B Thanks. Bye-bye.

4 A Unisex Hairdresser. Can I help you?
B Yes, please. I'd like an appointment to get my hair cut.
A One moment, please. Right. When would that be for?
B Have you got anything for tomorrow afternoon?
A I'm sorry, sir. We're all full for tomorrow. I can give you a time for the day after.
B That's Friday, isn't it?
A Yes, that's right.
B OK. So, er, what time then?
A Is six in the afternoon all right?
B Erm, yes, that sounds fine.
A And your name please?
B Oh, sorry, erm, David Taylor.
A Thank you, Mr Taylor. That's Friday 27th at six p.m.
B Thank you! Bye!

Irregular verbs

verb	past simple
be	was
	were
break	broke
buy	bought /bɔːt/
can	could /kʊd/
come	came
cut	cut
do	did
draw	drew
drink	drank
drive	drove
eat	ate
find	found
forget	forgot
get	got
give	gave
go	went
have	had
hear	heard /hɜːd/
know	knew /njuː/
learn	learnt
	learned
leave	left
lose	lost

verb	past simple
make	made
meet	met
put	put /pʊt/
read	read /red/
ring	rang
run	run
say	said /sed/
see	saw /sɔː/
sell	sold
send	sent
sing	sang
sit	sat
sleep	slept
speak	spoke
spend	spent
stand	stood /stʊd/
swim	swam
take	took /tʊk/
tell	told
think	thought /θɔːt/
understand	understood
wake up	woke up
wear	wore
write	wrote

« Look at the verb column. Cover the past simple column and test yourself.

OXFORD
UNIVERSITY PRESS

Great Clarendon Street, Oxford OX2 6DP

Oxford University Press is a department of the University of Oxford.
It furthers the University's objective of excellence in research, scholarship,
and education by publishing worldwide in

Oxford New York

Auckland Cape Town Dar es Salaam Hong Kong Karachi
Kuala Lumpur Madrid Melbourne Mexico City Nairobi
New Delhi Shanghai Taipei Toronto

With offices in

Argentina Austria Brazil Chile Czech Republic France Greece
Guatemala Hungary Italy Japan Poland Portugal Singapore
South Korea Switzerland Thailand Turkey Ukraine Vietnam

OXFORD and OXFORD ENGLISH are registered trade marks of
Oxford University Press in the UK and in certain other countries

ISBN: 978 0 19 430486 3

Printed in Portugal by Eigal

ACKNOWLEDGEMENTS

Illustrations by: Jo Bird/Jelly Illustration pp.55, 67; Emma Brownjohn/New
Division pp.6, 12, 14, 19, 28 top, 33, 36, 40 bottom, 47 left, 50, 53 bottom, 65
right; Clod/Comillus pp.11, 28 left, 29 right, 39, 46, 48 bottom, 54, 60, 64; Bob
Dewar p.23; Mark Duffin pp.4, 16, 18 left, 31, 35, 37, 47 right, 52 right, 56
right, 65 left, 69, 72; Helen Flook p.49; Pamela Goodchild via BL Kearley p.26
top; Glyn Goodwin pp.18 top, 24, 59; Simon Gurr p.57; Matt Johnstone/Jelly
Illustration pp.17, 26 bottom, 44, 56 left; George Onions pp.40 top, 71; Gavin
Reece pp.5, 25, 48 top; Mark Ruffle pp.10, 29 left, 34, 41 right, 53 top, 61, 62,
70; Phillip Warner p.43

*The Publishers and Author would also like to thank the following for permission to
reproduce photographs*: AKG p.51 (Paramount/Black Rain/Rear Window);
Anthony Blake Photolibrary pp.36 (Tim Hill/Risotto), 39 (Tim Hill/rice/risotto);
Corbis Images pp.15 (REUTERS/Ethan Mille/Sade), 45 (C. Lyttle/zefa/man and
grapes); Dawes p.68 (bicycles); DK Images p.36 (Spaghetti Bolognese, Russian
Salad); Empics pp.15 (Manu Fernandez/Ronaldinho, Claude Haller/Anastacia),
63 (Gurinder Osan); Getty Images pp.4 (Altrendo images/shaking hands), 21
(Lars Klove/hotel at night, Ryan McVay/hotel sitting room), 45 (PicturePress/
woman and dogs), 47 (Ken Weingart/couple with boy, Matthias Clamer/couple
with girl); iStockphoto p.22 (Velden/no vacancies sign); Ronald Grant Archive
p51 (Galaxie/Greenwich/Diva); Sally and Richard Greenhill pp.14 (c), 72 (Mark),
74 (Mark); Kobal Collection p.51 (UGC/Studio Canal/*Amelie*); Mercedes Benz
p.66; National Museum of Art, Architecture and Design, Oslo p.62; Oxford
University Press pp.4 (portraits), 7 (couple), 11, 12, 14 (a, b, d, e), 31, 36 (pasta,
meat, tomatoes, onion, cheese, potatoes, egg, yogurt, fish, peas, chicken,
rice, onion, carrots, salt), 42 (Bob, Lucy), 68 (Taj Mahal); Punchstock p.21
(bedroom); Rex Features pp.7 (Coldplay), 9, 15 (Ben Stiller, Stella McCartney),
20, 51 (*Snakes on a Plane*), 66 (old car); Zyro p.68 (bicycle accessories)

Recordings produced by: Leon Chambers